D1574827

*Rudolf Burger • Ernst Peter Brezovszky •
Peter Pelinka (Editors)*

GLOBAL ETHICS

Illusion or Reality?

With an Introduction by Benita Ferrero-Waldner

Rudolf Burger • Peter Brezovszky • Peter Pelinka (Editors)

GLOBAL ETHICS

Illusion or Reality?

With an Introduction by
Benita Ferrero-Waldner

CZERNIN VERLAG, VIENNA

Printed with the support of the Federal Ministry of Foreign Affairs, Cultural Policy Section.

Die Deutsche Bibliothek – CIP-Einheitsaufnahme
Burger, Rudolf - Brezovszky, Ernst Peter - Pelinka, Peter:
Global Ethics – Illusion or reality /Burger, Rudolf/Brezovszky,
Ernst Peter/ Pelinka, Peter
Vienna: Czernin Verlag, 2000
ISBN 3-7076-0041-6

The German edition was published in 1999, also by the Czernin Verlag, under the title "Ethik global – Illusion oder Realität". The present edition is funded by the Ferderal Ministry of Foreign Affairs and the School of Applied Art.

© 2000 by Czernin Verlag GmbH, Vienna
Cover: Bernhard Kerbl
Translation: V. I. T. A., Vienna Interpreting & Translation Agency
Typeset by Die Druckdenker GmbH, Vienna
Printed and bounded by Wiener Verlag, Himberg
ISBN 3-7076-0041-6

All rights reserved, including the rights to reproduce any part of this publication in print or electronic media.

Contents

Preface
ERNST-PETER BREZOVSZKY
Page 7

Introduction
BENITA FERRERO-WALDNER
Page 13

Towards an Open Society
GEORGE SOROS
Page 25

Global Ethics: Illusion and Reality
RUDOLF BURGER
Page 39

International Law versus the Rights of Man?
HANSPETER NEUHOLD
Page 63

A State as Work In Progress
HEDY FRY
Page 79

Nation State – Nation of State – National Minority
ARNOLD SUPPAN
Page 87

Thoughts on "Globalisation and
Global Ethics"
EBENEZER NJOH-MOUELLE
Page 97

Cultural Diversity at the National Level
BEATE WINKLER
Page 109

Globality, Global Ethics and Indigenous Dignity
SAKEJ YOUNGBLOOD HENDERSON
Page 119

Global Ethics in Practice
ANDREAS UNTERBERGER
Page 131

Informed to Death or Entertained to Death?
PETER PELINKA
Page 137

The World as a Global Living Room
ALEXANDER WRABETZ
Page 153

How Global are Global Values?
KRZYSZTOF ZANUSSI
Page 161

Globalisation Requires Cultural Dialogue
MONIKA KALISTA
Page 165

Vienna Conclusions on Globality and Global Ethics
Page 169

Authors
Page 173

Preface

Many people have a strikingly negative attitude to the world at the end of the 20th century: its general loss of values; the widening of the gap between rich and poor; technological possibilities that could increasingly undermine the rights of the individual and ultimately lead to a totalitarian all-controlling state; a total lack of any capacity for dialogue between cultures despite innovative communication technologies; demagogy and bloody conflicts, not to mention genocide. Just some of the items on a long list, and there is no doubt that many facts could be interpreted in this light. In the eyes of some analysts the merry apocalyptic spirit that prevailed at the close of the 19th century appears to be repeating itself, albeit this time around without the same upbeat spirit, even if a hundred years ago such a spirit was in appearance only.

However, this negative view of things does contrast with positive forecasts which, interestingly enough, point to quite different scenarios of the future based in part on the same social and technical outline conditions: a globalisation not just of the economy but also of the intellect; unfathomed opportunities to communicate world-wide using "information highways"; revolutionary new ways, unthinkable only a few years ago, for disadvantaged regions to access knowledge and education through new information technologies; the possibility of an open global society that is finally able to implement world-wide the ideas and ideals of the Enlightenment. All these factors herald a new pioneering spirit.

So are the opportunities and risks for an open and humane society today really closer than ever before in the history of humankind? There are plenty of indicators to support this notion. If so, there is an acute need for politics to take action, both at the national and the international level.

In June 1999, an international conference on the subject of "Global Ethics" took place at Vienna's Hofburg Palace at the initiative of the then Under-Secretary of State at the Austrian Federal Ministry of Foreign Affairs, Benita Ferrero-Waldner. This book, on the findings of the conference, aims to describe as many as possible of these fundamental issues that are shaping our age.

Rapid socio-technological progress versus a return to barbarism. World-wide opportunities for dialogue for all as opposed to resurgent nationalism and xenophobia in many regions of the world, including Europe. The general acceptance of the universality and indivisibility of human rights, contrasting admittedly with appalling shortfalls in their implementation. The utopia of global cultural and social pluralism based on mutual understanding and respect, with the crass contradiction of a renaissance in religious and socio-political fundamentalism that regards the word "dialogue" as nothing short of obscene. All these factors, like a compass needle caught in a magnetic field, do not particularly facilitate political action at the beginning of the new millennium. Today, in the global age, there is a more pressing need than ever before for political determination to shape our future. It presupposes a readiness to accept and take part in creating entirely new outline conditions.

At a conference entitled "Border-less?" in 1995, Johannes Rau, who has been Germany's Federal President since July 1999, stated the following:

"People today complain that our society no longer has a vision that makes conditions of survival the measure of present and future action. I could not disagree more! Ecological modernisation of industrial society is one such vision! Achieving it requires a new level of understanding between science, business and politics. If we take this to heart, we shall accomplish the great task of advancement that consists of combining what people are able to achieve with what they should be achieving, of closing the gap between their intellectual and their moral abilities.

Admittedly, it would be presumptuous and something of an excessive demand if politics were to set the time and tone for such an endeavour. Politics cannot improve people; it can, however, improve the social structures within which they live and work. That is why politicians must not arouse false hopes; rather, they must state openly what politics can and cannot achieve. We have no use for either delusions of omnipotence or airs of helplessness."

The individual essays in this book attempt to showcase different aspects of precisely this balancing act of politics between delusions of omnipotence and airs of helplessness. In her introduction State Secretary Ferrero-Waldner posits the basic considerations for her political initiative. This is followed by contributions from George Soros, financial expert; Hedy Fry, Canadian Secretary of State for Multi-

Cultural Affairs; Rudolf Burger, philosopher and Rector of the Vienna School of Applied Arts; Ebenezer Njoh-Mouelle, Cameroon Member of Parliament and philosopher; Hanspeter Neuhold, Viennese expert on international law; Sakej Youngblood Henderson, Canadian political expert of Indigenous roots; Beate Winkler, Director of the European Monitoring Centre on Racism and Xenophobia; Arnold Suppan, Viennese Eastern Europe historian and Director of the Austrian Eastern and South-Eastern European Institute; Krzysztof Zanussi, Polish film director; Monika Kalista, head of the foreign cultural policy department at the Austrian Ministry of Foreign Affairs; Andreas Unterberger and Peter Pelinka, editors-in-chief of two leading Austrian print media; and Alexander Wrabetz, business manager of Austrian TV and radio. Each author has chosen a different approach to the above issues. Some factual and analytical, others filled with emotional commitment.

Each of these authors addresses a basic problem: is it possible to contrast globalisation and its negative side-effects with a plausible and practicable global ethic? How compatible is a concept of universally applicable value standards with the call for cultural and social pluralism now widely seen as necessary? How can the international media contribute to the world-wide achievement and dissemination of pluralism, tolerance and mutual rapprochement? What is the rôle of culture, which throughout the history of mankind to the present day harbours the potential for both an understanding between nations and for racism and hatred of others?

As we address the issue of "Global Ethics" we must be aware

that virtually every answer will give rise to new dilemmas. This should not detract from the fact that we are dealing with one of the great issues of our times, one that will accompany us far into the next century. This book does not seek to provide trivial answers; indeed, we will have achieved a great deal if it succeeds in raising questions that give new constructive momentum to the globalisation debate. In any case we owe our thanks to the authors of the individual essays for the commitment with which they went about this difficult task.

Ernst-Peter Brezovszky,
Vienna, August 1999

Introduction

BENITA FERRERO-WALDNER

How should we lead our lives? Should we strive for happiness or knowledge, virtue or art? If we opt for happiness, should it be our own happiness or that of others? And what of insincerity? Is it right not to tell the truth in certain situations? Is it right for us to live in a society of excessive affluence while others are dying of hunger? If we have to fight a war that we do not support, is it right for us to disobey the law and act against it? What are our obligations to future generations?

These are just some of the questions whose answers we must seek in ethics. Ethics help mankind to take fundamental decisions; ethics also prescribe the standards by which mankind's actions may be judged as right or wrong.

In the age of globalisation the vision of a "global village" as initially formulated by Canadian author Marshall McLuhan no longer seems to us quite as startling. In fact, it has now become almost something of a platitude.

And yet, although we live in a "global village", we are confronted with an ever growing wave of new nationalism and chauvinism in the world. People are increasingly concerned about losing their identity, even though we have never before had so many opportunities to express ourselves and make ourselves heard by others.

While spoken and written words can now be "dashed" around the world within seconds, at an astonishing speed, many people appear lost for words and filled with aggression when faced with anything foreign.

Populist movements literally pounce on these fears and harness them often for evil purposes. It is the duty of responsible politicians to respond positively to this new situation. Never before in the history of mankind has the significance of dialogue – a genuine, profound dialogue that seeks to understand the ideas, ideals and concepts of others – been as crucial as it is today. Never before has dialogue between the North and the South, between the different cultures and legal concepts of the world been as important as it is today.

The global age requires an ability for dialogue between states as well as individuals. The days when one could choose between communicating with others and the possibility of complete isolation and reclusiveness are long gone. Today, to refuse dialogue is tantamount to hindering developments towards an open global society.

The globalisation of our planet has made the call for global ethics a priority. We live in an increasingly small world yet, at the same time, we must consider the phenomenon of an increasingly large world population. The need for a common world order to which we are all bound is no longer a luxury but a growing necessity of life, not to mention survival. The many years of ongoing tragedy in the Balkans is a vivid example. NATO's intervention in Kosovo clearly shows that the tenet of non-interference in national affairs set out by international law no longer applies in absolute terms. This conflict has highlighted the contradiction between the principle of the right of self-determination and the principle of territorial integrity and sovereignty of the state. At the same time it has shown that a continuing, serious violation of human rights will not be allowed to continue without counter-measures.

But that is not all. The Kosovo conflict has also shown that the contradictory interests of the Security Council's permanent members often prevent a resolution.

One does not have to be a pessimist to imagine future conflicts that will also be evaluated with widely differing views by the Security Council: the conflict between Russia and Chechnya, the border conflict between Pakistan and India, or the highly charged border relations between North and South Korea. Where, under what conditions and above all with what means should the international community of states intervene here?

In the years to come we shall be forced to address these issues in even greater detail.

However, these questions also show that through globalisation we are now dealing with a single global society. But does a global society not also warrant a global ethic? Does our global society not also demand a global law?

I believe these are some of the most topical issues of our times, and that is why I took the initiative for the "Global Ethics" conference. I wanted to set people's minds thinking and initiate an exchange of views. Moreover, it was important that a step be taken in this discussion process, which is undoubtedly still in its infancy.

Ethics always involve action; they act as guiding principles for our conduct, to make our lives together at the very least tolerable. In other words the ethical dimension begins as soon as an "Other" comes into play. Without the viewpoint of these "Others" we cannot grasp who we actually are.

Indeed, in his book "Belief or Non-Belief: A Confrontation", based on an exchange of correspondence with the Archbishop of Milan Carlo Maria Martini, Umberto Eco writes that "without the viewpoint and the response of others we cannot grasp who we are. Even he who kills, rapes, steals and wounds others does so only in moments of exception and spends the rest of his life seeking recognition, love, respect and praise from his peers". Ever since man has inhabited the planet, the issue of cohabitation and the right conduct, in other words ethics, have been a concern.

This concern has been reflected in approaches ranging from the Ten Commandments to the Torah, the Koran, the teachings of Buddha and Confucius, from Kant's categorical imperative to the resolutions and votes of the Security Council and the General Assembly of the United Nations.

In his book "The End of History" Francis Fukuyama sees the victory of democracy, human rights and the market economy over all other political systems as the outcome of political developments. In his opinion all will aspire in the Hegelian sense towards the state's highest possible level of development – namely the liberal, democratic state governed by the rule of law.

By contrast, Samuel Huntingdon believes we will be confronted by a massive rivalry between different ethical systems which sooner or later must lead to a clash of civilisations. By way of example he cites a fundamentalist and increasingly militant Islam.

These examples show that the search for global ethics is a problem both timeless and topical. Today, however, these issues have become more pressing that ever before.

In the following I would like to outline some of my own ideas on the subject.

First of all, I would like to take up a thought by Jean Jacques Rousseau, namely the idea of a link between politics and ethics: "Anyone who wishes to separate politics and ethics has failed to grasp any aspect of either".

Global ethics must always imply a political ethic. Nonetheless the age of globalisation has lent new significance and new urgency to achieving this goal. At the same time the changes in international outline conditions raise entirely new questions.

Nowadays the nation state, for so long the principal protagonist of political action, must first learn to live and deal with the presence of new players.

On the one hand the nation state has to address the development of supranational institutions, in which more and more powers are being vested on the other, the now stronger emphasis on the political formative power of regions and the ever increasing influence of the phenomenon of civil society on the formulation and implementation of politics.

All these developments involve new issues. For example: To whom precisely do we address calls for a global political ethic? The individual citizen? The region he perceives as his immediate home and which lends him an essential element of his identity? The nation state to which he is bound through ties of nationality? Supranational institutions which often still lack democratic legitimacy, having grown organically over time into nation-state institutions? Non-governmental organisations which today in certain cases sometimes have more possibilities of influencing political events than certain nation states? Or even all institutions with a possibility to shape political change?

When I talk of a "global" ethic, I believe I also have to ask the following fundamental question: Do these "global" terms actually exist? Are there elementary concepts that the human species as a whole shares in common and that can be expressed in all languages? It is not something that can be taken for granted by any means, given that there is a whole range of abstract concepts which while self-evident to us are totally unknown to many cultures.

Nonetheless I believe there are abstract concepts which all cultures have in common. To underline this point I refer to a semantic argument used by Umberto Eco in his aforementioned book "Belief or Non-Belief: A Confrontation": As human beings we all walk upright, which is why it is a strain for us to keep our heads down for any length of time; that is also why we have a shared concept of what is up and what is down, and why we prefer the former over the latter. Likewise we have a shared concept of a right-hand side and a left-hand side, of standing and lying, of being awake and being asleep.

This notion could be extended to include seeing, hearing, eating and drinking. And, no doubt, each one of us has a notion of what it means to perceive, to remember, to wish for, to be afraid, to be sad or relieved; what it means to utter sounds that express these feelings.

That is why we also have universal abstract concepts of compulsion: We do not want other people to prevent us from speaking, seeing, hearing, sleeping, travelling wherever we want. We suffer when we are tied up or locked away by others, beaten, wounded or killed, subjected to physical or mental torture.

More specifically: What exactly should the function of such "global ethics" be? Global ethics are not a new ideology or a new super-structure. Global ethics do not seek to make the specific ethos of the various religions and philosophies redundant.

Global ethics are not a substitute for the Torah, the Sermon on the Mount, the Koran, the discourses of Buddha or the wise words of Confucius. For me global ethics do not mean a single world culture, let alone a single world religion. Global ethics are not in any way a contradiction to the pluralism and diversity of our cultures, religions and history.

To me global ethics is the basic consensus, the necessary minimum of compulsory values, irrevocable standards and binding rules of behaviour, a common basis that can be embraced by all religions in spite of their dogmatic differences and also supported by non-believers. Given today's pressing political and social developments, such a basic consensus is necessary, not to say vital.

So how can our society achieve such a basic consensus? Here I would like to quote the Swiss theologian Hans Küng, who in his book "A Global Ethic for Global Politics and Economics", published in 1998, called for the following three points: A coalition between believers and non-believers in mutual respect; peace between civilisations; and peace between religions.

None of these three objectives can be reached without global dialogue, namely a dialogue between religions and civilisations, a dialogue between states and citizens. Nor can these objectives be reached without dialogue between the "First World" and the "Third World". As the member of the federal government responsible for development co-operation this dialogue is, naturally, particularly dear to my heart. It is the expression of our responsibility to and solidarity with the people of the Third World.

This "global dialogue" exists even if all too often it is blocked or obstructed by all manner of dogmatism, ideology and other prejudice. It is structured and conducted first and foremost within the framework of the United Nations and its specialist organisations. Its objective is to reach a consensus on the key questions of our lives together. It is a consensus science and technology cannot bring about; in fact they themselves depend on it. The great economic and technological problems of our time – and by this I mean essentially the complex problems that result from the "global economy" with its major multinational corporations, etc. – are often based on political and moral problems that require a basic ethical consensus.

A sceptic might say that the differences between nations, cultures, religions, ways of life, economic systems, social models and religious communities are so great that it is impossible to consider a basic ethical consensus. Yet no matter how diverse these national, cultural and religious differences may be, we are still dealing everywhere with people. And it is precisely these people who today are increasingly becoming a single community of fate through the modern means of communication of radio, television and the Internet.

So what should and could a basic ethical consensus consist of? In my opinion, of the respect of human rights as stated by the United Nations in the "Universal Declaration of Human Rights". For me the existence of this Declaration, which was signed by virtually all the nations of the world and last year celebrated its fiftieth anniversary, expresses the fact that global ethics already exist, at least in an initial form.

Critics will object that the Declaration of Human Rights is at best a moral appeal with limited effect. All one has to do is leaf through Amnesty International's annual report to see how often and how seriously human rights are violated and disregarded the Kosovo conflict referred to earlier is another case in point.

In my opinion it is now a matter of implementation: we already have a basic consensus on global ethics but we do not yet have a global law that we can implement. There is neither a global state, nor a global court, nor a global police force, and these institutions are not likely to come into being in the foreseeable future.

With the Yugoslav War Crimes Tribunal and the creation of an international criminal court, the international community has taken at least the first steps towards punishing the worst human rights violations such as genocide. It is to be hoped that those nations that have not yet declared their willingness to participate will join this consensus. The non-existence of an enforceable global law must not and should not lure us into sitting back and becoming idle bystanders while crimes and inhuman injustices are committed.

Ethics mean action, and apply first and foremost to the individual, to each person. On the basis of this global ethic the individual has both the opportunity and the duty to take action.

The following examples demonstrate that the commitment of individuals is not in vain or senseless:

• Without the unselfish involvement of someone such as Henry Dunant and the small Geneva committee that sought to alleviate the sufferings of war, would the Geneva Convention of 1864 and the founding of the Red Cross ever have occurred, an institution which today is active in 150 countries around the world – even as the Red Crescent?

• Without the political vision of a Woodrow Wilson or a Franklin Delano Roosevelt, would the League of Nations and the United Nations ever have come about?

- Without Andrei Sacharov and other Russian dissidents, would the collapse of the Soviet Union ever have happened?
- Without Vaclav Havel and other civil rights activists, would a new Europe ever have emerged?
- Without the vision of a Hermann Gmeiner, would SOS Kinderdörfer ever have been established?

Of course we are all well aware of the objections of the sceptics, who maintain that the actions of the Red Cross, SOS Kinderdörfer and other humanitarian organisations are often merely a drop in the ocean; that the League of Nations was an obvious failure and proved unable to prevent the Second World War; that the United Nations itself has failed in many instances and was unable, in Rwanda for example, to halt the killing and the murdering, and was unable to improve the situation of the Kurds and the Shiites in Iran, etc.; that to this day the Declaration of Human Rights has not prevented the constant violation of human rights in China, Tibet, Burma, Israel, Palestine and Kosovo, etc.

This is all true and it sometimes makes scepticism and pessimism seem justified. And yet, it should not and must not prevent us from doing what is good and right in the light of the Human Rights Declaration. The Universal Declaration of Human Rights could become the Magna Carta of the 20th and 21st centuries. Whether or not this happens will, I am quite certain, depend ultimately not just on the international community of states but on each and everyone of us. It will depend on whether we are prepared to stand up for human rights and for justice, and whether we put up resistance wherever these fundamental rights are violated.

The debate about "global ethics" is also an opportunity

to think about all the pessimistic predictions we hear time and time again, especially this year, the last year of our century and millennium. I would refer here to Sir Karl Popper, who spoke out in favour of the positive, of the fact that every history has always found a new beginning. Indeed, history is not a linear process.

We, too, are called upon and capable, today, in 1999, of making a fresh start, and for this a "global ethic" is essential. Our thinking should be characterised not by panic-mongering in the face of the unknown, of the "Other", but by openness and humanitarianism; to quote Hans Jonas: "We will only know what is at stake once the chips are down".

Today, there is a great deal at stake; most importantly of all, peace.

That is why global ethics must also be political ethics. Indeed, to be a "great politician" or a "great entrepreneur" one needs not only analytical skills and the power of decision-making but also a vision that goes beyond specialist knowledge, that sees the overall picture and senses the fundamental questions of mankind, as well as well-founded ethical convictions - i.e. a "global ethic".

Towards an Open Society

George Soros

The title of this conference is: Global ethics: illusion or reality?

After the Kosovo crisis, there can be no doubt that global ethics is a reality. NATO intervened in the name of global ethics. Milosevic's policy towards Kosovo could not be tolerated. There were no national interests involved, only fundamental values. But the outcome of the intervention was very different from what was intended. The horror of the bombing raised some questions about global ethics as it is currently practiced – in my mind and in many others'. We need to address these questions if we want global ethics to prevail, as I do.

I am a believer in what I call an open society. Open society is basically a broader and more universal concept of democracy. The concept of the open society is based on the recognition that nobody has access to the ultimate truth; perfection is unattainable and therefore we must be satisfied with the next best thing: a society that holds itself open to improvement. An open society allows people with different views, identities and interests to live together in peace.

An open society transcends boundaries; it allows intervention in the internal affairs of sovereign states because people living in an oppressive regime often cannot defend themselves against oppression without outside intervention, but the intervention must be confined to supporting the people living in a country to attain their legitimate aspirations, not to impose a particular ideology or to subjugate one state to the interests of another. These are the principles I have sought to put into practice through my network of open society foundations.

Guided by these principles I have no doubt that Milosevic infringed the rights of the Albanian population in Kosovo. Nor do I have any doubts that the situation required outside intervention. The case for intervention is clearer in Kosovo than in most other situations of ethnic conflict because Milosevic unilaterally deprived the inhabitants of Kosovo of the autonomy they had already enjoyed. He also broke an international agreement into which he had entered in October of last year. My doubts center on the ways in which international pressure was applied.

I found the spectacle of NATO planes dropping bombs from high altitudes profoundly disturbing and I was afraid that it was accomplishing exactly the opposite of what was intended. We accelerated the ethnic cleansing we sought to interdict and we made it more difficult for people in Serbia to oppose the Milosevic regime. We destabilized the neighboring countries of Montenegro, Macedonia and Albania, not to mention the broader international complications such as our relationship with China.

I was an avid supporter of a firm line against Milosevic and I felt a personal sense of responsibility for the consequences. I am delighted that Milosevic caved in before the unity of NATO disintegrated and I breathed a profound sigh of relief. Relief but not relish.

We have taken a giant step forward towards establishing the principle of intervening in the internal affairs of a sovereign country in order to protect its people, but we cannot be satisfied with the results. NATO intervention in Kosovo, instead of unifying the world behind that principle, has profoundly divided it. Even I, who have been guided by that principle, have come to have my doubts about it.

I have been forced to ask myself: is it possible, is it appropriate to intervene in the internal affairs of a state in the name of some general principle like human rights or open society? I did not want to consider such a question and I certainly don't want to accept no for an answer. It would be the end of my aspiration to an open society. In the absence of outside intervention oppressive regimes could perpetrate untold atrocities. Moreover, internal conflicts could easily broaden into international hostilities. In our increasingly interdependent world, there are certain kinds of behavior by sovereign states – aggression, terrorism, ethnic cleansing – that cannot be tolerated by the international community. At the same time we must recognize that our current approaches do not work. In the case of Yugoslavia we have intervened in different ways. In Bosnia we tried it with the United Nations and it didn't work. That is why in Kosovo we tried it without the United Nations and that didn't work very well either. We also tried it by applying economic sanctions but that too had adverse consequences. The sanctions could be broken by shady businessmen operating with the help of the ruling regimes. This led to the emergence of a Mafioso type business community which was in cahoots with the ruling regimes not only in Yugoslavia but also in the neighboring countries. In short, nothing worked. And we have a similar record in Africa.

We must find some better way. This will require a profound rethinking and reorganization of the way we conduct international relations, what we may call the global security architecture.

It may be too early to start such a discussion. Emotions are running high, including my own. Opinions are sharply divided and each side is too concerned to vindicate its own position to be able to take a more dispassionate view. But, I don't think it is too early. I believe I am not the only advocate of intervention who has been shaken by the consequences. I believe there is a general recognition that something is woefully wrong in the current state of affairs and we must do something about it. It takes a crisis to bring about a change in the global security architecture: the League of Nations was created after the First World War and the UN after the Second. If we have been sufficiently shocked by the Kosovo conflict, we can perhaps bring about some changes in the global security architecture which will prevent a Third World War. If we simply declare victory, I believe Kosovo will have brought us closer to it. We must start with the recognition that security depends not merely on what happens between states but also on what happens within states. A repressive regime can pose a threat not only to its own people, but also to its neighbors and to the world at large. The country concerned does not need to be as strong as Nazi Germany was. It can be as weak as Iraq or Yugoslavia or even Rwanda.

The principles which ought to govern the behavior of states towards their own citizens have been reasonably well-established. Those are the principles of democracy, or in my terminology: open society.

What is missing is an authority to enforce those principles – an authority that transcends the sovereign state. Sovereignty may be an outdated concept but it prevails, except in those rare cases where it has been explicitly surrendered.

Sovereignty derives from the time when kings wielded

power over their subjects. In the French Revolution the people of France overthrew their king and they assumed his sovereignty. That was the birth of the modern state. Since then, there has been a gradual recognition that states must also be subject to the rule of law but international law has been slow to develop and it does not have any teeth.

We have the Universal Declaration of Human Rights and we have the United Nations but the UN does not work well because it is an association of states, many of which are not democratic.

Since the sovereignty of the modern state is derived from the people, the authority that transcends the sovereign state must be derived from the people of the world. As long as we live in a world of sovereign states, the people need to exercise their authority through the states to which they belong, particularly where military action is concerned.

Democratic states are supposed to carry out the will of the people. So in the ultimate analysis the development and enforcement of international law depends on the will of the people who live in democratic countries.

And that is where the problem lies. People who live in democratic countries do not necessarily believe in democracy as a universal principle. They tend to be guided by self-interest, not by universal principles. They may be willing to defend democracy in their own country because they consider it to be in their own self-interest but few people care sufficiently about democracy as an abstract idea to defend it in other countries, especially when the idea is so far removed from the reality.

Many countries are not democratic and even those which are have very different views on what democracy means. In a sense, the Milosevic regime's policy towards Kosovo has had the support of the people and it was his Kosovo policy that helped him to attain power and to hold on to it.

I used to believe that the concept of an open society could provide an adequate basis for a global security architecture because it entails not only democracy but also some generally agreed standards of behavior. Milosevic, for instance, does not qualify.

The concept of an open society certainly provided me and my foundations with an almost unerring sense of direction. Events have forced me to recognize, however, that the concept suffers from a built-in deficiency. It is valid only if people believe in it. I call it the paradox of the open society. If people do not care for the principles of the open society, an open society cannot prevail. This holds true even within the state; it applies with much greater force to international relations where many states are not democratic to start with.

The paradox does not invalidate the concept of an open society. On the contrary, it makes the concept self-consistent. After all, an open society is based on the recognition that the ultimate truth is beyond our reach. But it does make it much harder to build a global security architecture on the concept.

First, it would require general agreement that an open society is a desirable objective; second, it would require some consensus on what an open society entails. And finally, it would require some institutions to implement the agreed goals. The third requirement is the most crucial one because it is the institutions that define their goals and their methods of implementation.

The most obvious candidate for building an open society would be the UN but it is not suitable for the task because it is an association of states, some of which are democratic, others not, each of which is guided by its national interests. As it is currently constituted, it can do many things but it cannot build an open society. The task can only be accomplished by an alliance of democratic states which subscribe to the principles of open society.

As it happens, we have such an alliance, NATO. And NATO did intervene in Yugoslavia.

But NATO is a military alliance incapable of preventive action. By the time it intervenes it is too late and we have seen that its intervention can be counterproductive.

Both logic and experience indicate that an open society cannot be imposed by military means. Military intervention may be necessary but it cannot be sufficient to build an open society. Building is a constructive activity. NATO as a military alliance needs to be complemented by a political alliance dedicated to the promotion of open society. That is what is missing from today's security architecture.

NATO as an institution is left over from the cold war. When it was adapted to the post-communist era a fatal mistake was made: it was expanded geographically, but it was not adapted to the conditions of the post-communist era. It was not recognized that the main security threat in the post-communist world comes from what happens within states, not what happens between states. And it is still not sufficiently recognized.

I have attended a number of discussions about Kosovo and I was shocked how vague and confused people, well-informed people, are about the reasons for our involvement. They speak of humanitarian reasons and human rights almost interchangeably. Yet the two are quite different. Human rights are political rights. When they are violated, it may lead to humanitarian disaster, pictures on CNN that arouse people's emotions but by then it is too late. The damage is done and the intervention is often counterproductive. The humanitarian disaster could have been prevented only by protecting the political rights of the people. But to achieve this, people must take an interest in the political rights of other people. Prevention cannot start early enough. To be successful it must be guided by the principles of an open society.

A political alliance devoted to building an open society would work more by providing incentives for good behavior than punishment for bad behavior. Belonging to the alliance or meeting its standards should be a rewarding experience. This would encourage voluntary compliance and defer any problems connected with the infringement of national sovereignty. The first degree of punishment would be exclusion; only if it fails need other measures be considered.

The greatest rewards would be access to markets, access to finance, better treatment by the international financial institutions and, where appropriate, association with the European Union.

There are a thousand little ways that diplomatic pressure can be applied; the important thing is to be clear about the objectives. I am sure that the abolition of Kosovo's autonomy in 1989 could have been reversed if the international community had been determined enough about it.

In Latvia, international pressure had led to a reform of the naturalization law and a potential conflict with Russia is being defused.

In Slovakia, international support for mobilizing civil society has resulted in the defeat of Meciar.

In Croatia, the international community has not done

enough to assure the existence of independent media and Tudjman is still in power.

Nor is the international community sufficiently aroused by proposals in various Central Asian republics to introduce lifetime presidencies.

We may not be able to get rid of Milosevic by bombing but if, after the war, there is a grand plan for the reconstruction of South East Europe involving a customs union and virtual membership in the EU for those countries which are not ruled by an indicted war criminal, I am sure that the Serbs will soon get rid of Milosevic in order to qualify.

We must be realistic: carrots don't always work.

In 1990 before the breakup of Yugoslavia, the European community offered 3 billion ECU in aid if only Yugoslavia would stay together in one piece; but it did not prevent the breakup of Yugoslavia. Sometimes it is necessary to resort to force. That is where NATO comes in; but it ought to be the last resort. Intervention is the failure of prevention.

We can consider ourselves fortunate that the military intervention has been successful and Milosevic has acceded to minimum NATO demands. It reaffirms the military might of NATO. But might is not right. It merely gives us another chance to do the right thing. We now have a wonderful opportunity to make up for past mistakes and do something positive, both in the Balkans and also more generally.

We must stop reacting to crises and embark on a proactive, constructive program of development not only for Kosovo but for the entire region of South East Europe.

I don't use the term Balkans because many people in the Balkans don't want to belong to the Balkans. But they all want to belong to Europe and the European Union could work wonders by embracing them.

Ethnic conflicts cannot be resolved by ethnic cleansing or by the adjustment of borders. They can be resolved only by diminishing the importance of borders and establishing the principles of open society. The European Union can offer the carrots that will attract people to this solution.

A think tank in Brussels called CEPS has produced an imaginative program which amounts to a kind of Marshall Plan for South East Europe. The experience with Bosnia has shown that the individual entities are too small to be developed individually.

The key ideas in the CEPS plan are to abolish the customs barriers between the individual entities, give them access to the European Common Market, introduce the EURO as the common currency and to compensate the governments for the loss of customs revenue and the loss of segneurage.

The total amount made available would be in the region of 5 billion EURO annually. This amount would fit into the Europe 2000 agreement reached in Berlin.

Customs are a major source of corruption; the same applies to other forms of regulation. At the same time, an open society requires the rule of law. The amount of aid given to individual governments would be conditional on their performance.

Again, judging by the experience in Republica Srpska, I am sure that Yugoslavia would soon get rid of Milosévic and present an acceptable face in order to qualify for the aid.

Needless to say, I am strongly in favor of such a program.

I have been arguing in favor of carrots ever since the Soviet Empire started to crumble. I urged a Marshall Plan for the Soviet Union in the spring of 1989 at a meeting in Potsdam when Potsdam was still in East Germany and my proposal was literally met with laughter – "Heiterkeit" as the Frankfurter Allgemeine Zeitung called it. At the time when NATO expansion was first mooted, I suggested that the partnership for peace ought to be complemented by a partnership for prosperity.

I want to conclude by making a few remarks about the new global security architecture.

In the first instance an open society alliance must start with the members of NATO and those members of the partnership for peace which subscribe to the principles of an open society.

The European Union needs a joint security policy, yet the member states did not surrender their sovereignty rights to the European Union in the Maastricht Agreement. The Union should speak with a single voice and has at last found this voice in the person of Javier Solana. The question as to what issues the European Union should address and what should be left to the competence of the individual states has not yet been answered. Many aspects of foreign policy are within the sphere of competence of the individual states, for example trade relations with various Asian countries.

Other subjects such as the problem in Kosovo were actually not really matters of national interests of the individual member states. It was definitely in the interest of the European Union to resolve this conflict. In any talk of these EU interests, it should be noted that they are not confined to Europe, for these were also matters that concerned both the United States and Canada.

A political organization that works together with NATO

would be the proper framework to handle such matters, a framework within which the individual states would have to surrender their sovereignty to permit effective action. If I look further into the future of this alliance for an open society, I would say that it ought to unite all democratically minded nations in the world. It would then have sufficient legitimacy to be able to act both within the United Nations and outside it. The question as to what extent the United Nations should be reformed is beyond the scope of this essay. A number of reform attempts have been made; all have failed. An alliance of this kind might really be able to reform the United Nations and for the very reason that it would be able to act within the UN and outside it. But at this stage, all of this is merely a pipe dream.

I realize that such an alliance for an open society would require a radical change of attitudes particularly in the United States. The US is caught in a trap of its own making. It used to be one of the two superpowers and the leader of the free world. It is now the sole remaining superpower and it would like to think of itself as the leader of the free world. But that is where it fails, because it fails to observe one of the basic principles of the open society. Nobody has a monopoly on the truth, yet it acts as if it did. It is willing to violate the sovereignty of other states in the name of universal principles but it is unwilling to accept any infringement of its own sovereignty. It is willing to drop bombs on others from high altitudes but it is reluctant to expose its own men to risk. It refuses to submit itself to any kind of international governance. It was one of seven countries which refused to subscribe to the International Criminal Court; the others were China, Iraq, Libya, Qatar and Yemen. It does not even pay its dues to the United Nations.

This kind of behavior does not lend much legitimacy to its claim to be the leader of the free world.

To reclaim that role the US must radically alter its attitude to international cooperation. It cannot and should not be the policeman of the world; but the world needs a policeman. Therefore the US must cooperate with like-minded countries and abide by the rules that it seeks to impose on others. It cannot bomb the world into submission but it cannot withdraw into isolation either. My hope is that the political leadership in the US as well as the other democracies are as shocked by what has happened in Yugoslavia as I am.

It takes a crisis to bring about a change in attitudes.

Kosovo ought to have been a big enough crisis to force us to reconsider how we conduct international relations. If not, we are doomed to face bigger crises.

Global Ethics: Illusion and Reality

Rudolf Burger

I.

In 1947, the leading phenomenologist Maurice Merleau-Ponty wrote the following in his great essay "Humanism and Terror", in response to a debate on the terror of Stalinism, which had been put on the agenda of Western intellectual debate by Arthur Koestler's novel "Darkness at Noon":

"(The discussion) does not consist of examining whether communism adheres to the rules of liberal thinking (for it is all too obvious that it does not) but whether the power it exercises is revolutionary and capable of establishing human relations between people. The Marxist critique of the liberal concept is so strong that one would have to be communist if, through world revolution, communism were about to establish a classless society in which the causes of war and decadence had disappeared, along with the exploitation of man by man (…). Is communism up to its humanistic intentions? That is the real question."[1]

No-one nowadays would ever write or speak in those terms. Today, we are so certain of a negative reply to Merleau-Ponty's question that even posing the question seems ridiculous, and the instrumental relationship to power and the dissolution of the moral code in politics also appears

---

[1] M. Merleau-Ponty, Humanism and Terror, 1969

almost obscene. In 1947, however, the year of the Truman Doctrine, at the beginning of the Cold War, Merleau-Ponty could still raise the question of the moral code as an openly political question, in other words he was discussing it within the framework of an historical-philosophical essay. The fact *that* he was discussing it at all rather than simply attributing it to ideological forms as Marx has done is an indication in itself that teleological certainty had become brittle, a certainty which in Koestler's novel still determined the actions of both Gletkin *and* Rubashov. After all, the latter's tragedy resides in the fact that he has to sentence himself according to his own principles for he has strayed from the correct line as a result of political error. Thus the moral code comes into play only *ex negativo*. For the functionary and militant who sees himself as the executor of an historical tendency, the moral code has slipped into both the transcendental and into historical transcendence; as a means of regulating empirical practice, it shows a tendency to be invalidated: the moral code determines itself according to strategic calculations just as that of his adversary always had and he, too, had put the moral precept to tactical use. However, as an impulse the moral code *precedes* his actions, which in turn are intended to establish a situation which, being inherently moral, no longer requires a moral means of regulation – this however implies a departure from existing structures and therefore does not exclude the use of violence.

"When good and evil are once again incorporated into the times and blend with events, then nothing is either good or evil any longer but simply too soon or too late. Who can decide about opportunity if not the opportunist? Later you can sit in judgement, say the followers. But the victims are no longer there to sit in judgement. For the victim the present is the only value," wrote Albert Camus in 1952 countering Merleau-Ponty's historical perspective of political morals[2]. The figure of the "opportunist" is highly discredited and Camus, too, uses the term "opportunist" in a pejorative sense. And yet every politician is an opportunist if he is not a fool or a dreamer in wich case he is not a politician at all but either an ideological missionary or a political fanatic. For the stringent moralist pragmatic politics are always immoral, as they are for those who see politics as the execution of an historical "purpose". Those who, as the saying goes, wanted to "make history", negated concrete morals yet did so in the name of an ever more stringent abstract moral code. These are the dialectics Camus had in mind when he wrote the following sentences in the same work, in "L'Homme révolté" ("The Rebel").

"Historical thinking should free man from his subservience to God yet this liberation demands from him a complete subservience to the process of becoming. One then runs to the party office just as one prostrated oneself before the altar. For this reason the age that dares to refer to itself as being in wildest revolt offers only the choice between several forms of conformism. The true passion of the 20th century is servitude."

And that is why the German original title of Koestler's novel, now lost to us, is not "Darkness at Noon" but "Circulus vitiosus" - for there is no escape from the logic of historical judgement because it is the moral judgement itself that one plays off against it, in an extremely radicalised form.

---

[2] A. Camus, The Rebel: An Essay on Man in Revolt

Since 1789 at the latest, revolutionaries have pled that they are in fact seeking to establish genuine relationships of law, that they did not invent violence, rather that violence already existed and was now being turned against its real perpetrators. Paradigmatic in this sense is Saint-Just, who advocated terror as a means to virtue (in a speech on the ventôse decrees for example), and of course above all Robespierre, who in his great speech "On the Principles of Political Morals" (1794) specifically declared terror as the outflow of virtue ("it flows out of virtue" as he literally put it).

Given that these men themselves acted out of virtue, it was a consistent step for, as Hegel wrote, to virtue "law is what is essential, and individuality what is to be eliminated". To abstractly reject its abstract violence, as conventional morals require, means condemning the objective with its means character, an objective which consists in the abolition of violent circumstances. In other words, the amorality of the political militant is merely morality thought through to its end.

Any political action is inevitably both *praxis* and *poisis*, dealing with people as subjects and their degradation to the material. He who wishes to reduce it to *praxis* and "bind" it morally is either a hypocrite or someone who knows not what he is saying. Never to use the other *merely* as a means, as the Kantian imperative requires in one of its versions, means admitting that he is always *also* a means, and the further removed the situation aimed for actually is from the current situation, the more this moment will come to the fore. To the extent to which action sees itself as historical, it cancels out moral judgement in the political.

Post-Kantian philosophy turned against the abstract virtue of middle-class revolution. Revolutionary action now seeks its justification in the philosophy of history, not in the timeless commandments of the moral code, and conversely declares those commandments to be an ideological system and subjects them to strategic calculation. This idea of history as a process of liberation has shaped history for more than a century and, until recently, split the world into two camps. And the commitment to, or at least silent support for, one of the two camps gave individuals – and more particularly the most enlightened and most aware among them – that which they needed most in a post-religious and post-metaphysical age: a goal in life and something of an overarching "purpose" that justified their existence. Thus the party man became the predominant social figure of an entire century.

The great Russian-French exponent of Hegel, Alexander Kojève, whose seminars on the "phenomenology of the intellect" in the thirties were attended by virtually all the subsequent great minds of French philosophy, regarded both camps – the middle-class capitalist camp on the one hand and the proletarian communist camp on the other – as politically practical derivations of Hegelian philosophy, whose struggle, whether consciously or not, should determine the correct interpretation of the text. There was, as Kojève characterises the state of the inwardly disrupted spirit of absolutism after 1831, i.e. after Hegel's death, "from the very outset an Hegelian Left and an Hegelian Right, but that was *also* all there had been since Hegel" – where "Hegelian Left" is merely a capricious term for revolutionary Marxism. Because it was of such historical consequence Marxist philosophy was the only philosophy taken seriously; in consequence of Hegelianism it promised a higher principle as the telos of history than the liberal, middle-class capitalist constitutional state:

"If one disregards the relicts of the past, which were known to Hegel and have been described by him (including "liberalism") and therefore cannot be submitted to him as historical or "dialectic" refutations, then one realises that, strictly speaking, there has not been anything other than Hegelianism (consciously or not), neither at the level of historical reality itself nor at the level of thinking and rhetoric, that would have had an historical repercussion. Therefore one cannot (...) say that history has refuted Hegelianism. At most one might claim that it has not yet decided between its "leftist" and its "rightist" interpretation of Hegelian philosophy. (...) After Hegel a discussion can only be decided through reality, i.e. through the realisation of one of the two adversarial theses. The verbal polemics or "dialectics" merely reflect the real dialectics, which is a dialectics of action which manifests itself as struggle and labour. And for almost 150 years, in labour ("economic system"), revolutions and wars, the polemic has been played out between "Hegelians" (...) History (will) never refute Hegelianism; it will simply content itself with choosing between its two opposite interpretations".

Kojève wrote the above in 1946, at a time when the two interpretations, now a reality, faced one another bluntly as "blocs". At the ideological level both blocs represented a universalistic moral code yet neither was universal; instead they were merely regionally limited to their respective spheres of power and influence: the *human rights universalism* of the "free world" opposed to the *proletarian universalism* of the communist world; in their regional limitation, they negated each other, each claiming global power and validity for themselves. Driven upwards in a Manichaean spiral the decision remained open, history having not yet chosen between the rival interpretations of its Hegelian text. Today, after 1989 and the collapse of communism, Kojève, were he still alive, would say that history had made its decision and opted for the rightist variant of its interpretation. The liberal capitalistic principle has won and essentially become universal as the supreme principle of socio-economic organisation. The rest is a matter of formulation, differentiation and dissemination, if necessary by force, at worse a partial relapse to earlier, more primitive levels of social order, for instance fascism or religious fundamentalism, here again nothing new. There is no sign, however, of a higher principle than the secularised, middle-class liberal constitutional state with mass democracy and a separation of powers based on a capitalistic economy, somewhat softened by the welfare state, ecologically supplemented and a little embellished through art in architecture. The whole arrangement calls itself "cultural society", and rightly so. It is the adequate habitat for the figure which Nietzsche calls the "last man", who has found happiness within himself and stands there, blinking with astonishment: for the struggles which, since the beginning of the 19th century, were – consciously or not – struggles for the correct interpretation of a text are over. And with it history as a history of the struggle for a principle which began in the 19th century as a communist utopia…

That and nothing else is the true core of the literally market-stall clamour surrounding the central thesis of "The End of History", launched a few years ago both colourfully and plagiaristically by Francis Fukuyama, in the wake of Kojève. But of course history does go on, as a history of events; Kojève knew this, Fukuyama knows this and so of course did Arnold Gehlen, who in the fifties had already coined the term *posthistoire*; what the thesis claims is not the end of empirical history but its end as a concept and as a project; it maintains the end of the age of the philosophy of history and its post-religious functions as a dispenser of comfort and meaning. The politics oriented philosophy of history was after all an attempt to tame real history and to subject it to a human purpose. The fact that history post-1989 is turbulently clearing a path for itself everywhere, not just in the post-communist countries, is not an argument against finalism but for it: *posthistoire* is the liberation of history – from the claim of knowing how it should be made. As Marx had already observed, history still goes on as a natural process – admittedly without our sharing his hope that we could ever control it as a process, for that hope has proved a totalitarian illusion.

The "project of modernity" (J. Habermas), if it ever was one, is in principle completed: as a nihilistic libertarian mass democracy.

The reason I refer to it as "nihilistic" is that it no longer has a metaphysical roof over its head to afford it an absolute meaning pillared on the transcendental – the talk of "moral values" alone points in this direction: the concept of "value" is, after all, originally an economic one and was imported into moral philosophy only in the late 19th century by Lotze and others, and popularised by Nietzsche; and because it no longer has a positive historical goal before it, its function is more negative and critical: it lies in fending off the constant threat of totalitarian systems of purpose that threaten both morally and politically the human rights universalism of the capitalistic world system. That is, indeed, the militant core of meaning of Popper's concept of "the open society", which will certainly have to express itself in militant terms.

II.

But no matter how large-scale the carnage for the "preservation of values" may be, from an Hegelian point of view it is insignificant; it now merely safeguards the status quo and all is no longer at stake. During the nuclear poker game of the Cold War, the existence of the species as a whole was at stake. Now the "battle of values" has been decided: the principle of "freedom", the human rights universalism, the moral expression of liberal-democratic capitalism, has carried the day historically over the principle of "equality", proletarian internationalism, the moral expression of egalitarian dictatorial communism – and ironically it has done so according to strict Marxist logic. For it was the "shackling of productive resources" that caused the communist means of production to collapse; the collapse was caused endogenously, without the need for military intervention from the outside; the competitive rivalry between the systems and the policy of containment were sufficient.

Thus the logic of values was able to develop purely, with both "freedom" and "equality" introduced into the world by the French Revolution, the violent birth of political modernity, as supreme political principles. The struggle of "freedom" versus "equality" determined in unadulterated form the confrontation of powers during the Cold War, mobilised antagonistically against one another, through the intermediary of the principle of "fraternity", a principle often overlooked in the theory or belittled for its alleged lack of seriousness yet in reality the most appalling principle in the revolutionary trinity.

Indeed, unlike the universalism of "freedom" and "equality", "fraternity" is a politically marginalising principle of collectivisation: allied to the principle of "freedom" it creates "ethnos", the ideological collective community of the nation-state founded on mass democracy; allied to the principle of "equality", it creates "class", the ideological collective community of revolutionary party dictatorships. In both combinations it plays a serving role, activating in political terms either the "citizen" or the "comrade". Taken in isolation, it establishes the "community of the people", i.e. the nationalistic ideology of fascism. Indeed, one should not be deceived by the cosy ring of the familial metaphor but take note of its denotative core meaning: it refers as much to the consanguinity of a clan as the term "nation" which, derived from "natio", designates the blood-related unity of a national body; that is why both terms are at least latently racist. The promise that "all mankind shall be brothers..." is in reality a threat of a fascist universal state – which being universal would of course no longer be a state.

Liberalism, communism and fascism: the three historically new, mutually hostile forms of society that are characteristic of modernity are the politically crystallised achievements of the three revolutionary principles of freedom, equality and fraternity.

The victory of the liberal principle was total and with it human rights universalism became hegemonic – which does not mean that in some backward regions "fraternity" did not lie dormant, to be roused here and there as a fundamentalist ideology of community and separation against the cold dynamics of freedom; any religion, not just Islam, provides the corresponding "values".

III.

But even if human rights universalism were recognised world-wide in fact – and not just as a declamatory principle – as a basis of values for "global ethics", it would not by any means signify that the battles were over, neither the social struggles within a societal development structured as a state, nor the conflicts between states. As history teaches us, they can take place just as well on a common basis of values as between rival value systems – were that not so there should never have been bloody conflicts in the "Christian West", or, if there were, no more than the few the Islamic Word, for example, experienced. In reality, the opposite is true – the "Crusades" tend to be the exception while intra-cultural conflicts are the rule: common interests create animosities – a fact that holds true both ideologically and geographically. As much as he may have been right in other respects the one serious flaw of Samuel Huntington's "Clash of Civilisations"[3] is not to have given due respect to this observation. What matters is never the "world views" and the value systems inherent to them as such but their specific, interest-driven interpretations in each case. That is why for instance the confessional civil wars of the 16th and 17th centuries, among the bloodiest and most devastating ever experienced in Europe and out of which there emerged the modern secular state as a neutralising body, were referred to for good

---

[3] S. Huntington, The Clash of Civilizations, in: Foreign Affairs 72/3 (Summer 1993), page 22 - 49

reason as "hermeneutic civil wars" for they took place on the common basis of Christian values; ideologically they revolved around the correct interpretation of commonly recognised canonical texts. A similar observation can be made in respect of all the factional power struggles within political parties as a so-called "ideological camp"; these battles are often fought much more ruthlessly than those between the parties themselves.

And of course the same holds true for human rights universalism, which emerged the victor from the "great contest" (Isaak Deutscher) against proletarian internationalism. Indeed, it would be naïve to trace the growing influence of universalistic ethics back to a "moral improvement of the human race" (I. Kant) – or conversely to expect any such improvement from those ethics. What might change are the front-line positions and certainly the forms of legitimation but definitely not the number nor the intensity of the conflicts, other things being equal. Indeed, that is why Immanuel Kant referred to the theorists of international law as "nothing but tiresome consolers".

It may well be – and I believe it to be so – that the codified universalism of human rights, and any "global ethics" as such, originates from the subjectively honourable and commendable intention to shape the world according to ethical principles in the wake of this century's bitter experiences, and to rein in politics with moral criteria. Nevertheless the case in the past has always been that in the interplay between the ethical and the political it is the ethical that has submitted to the logic of the political – what's more, the reasons for actually mobilising the ethical were primarily political in nature. And nothing else can be expected as long as politics exists as a separate sphere of action, in other words as long as mankind lives in partially organised interest groups forced to hold their ground against the outside. Such groups do not necessarily have to be states, communities of states or state-like entities, as is the case today and probably will continue to be for the foreseeable future. "The concept of state presupposes the concept of the political," says Carl Schmitt; and not vice versa.

Whatever the inside view of a moral code may be – whether it has settled as a self-evident moral substance, become a "hexis" as Aristotle put it, whether it is a well-intended norm or merely a hypocritically simulated maxim for action, any outside sociological view will always reveal its political function.

Accordingly, one can interpret human rights along with, for example, MacPherson as the battle cry of the propertied middle-classes or view them – like Niklas Luhmann – as a means of dismantling corporative society as a transitional state towards a societal form structured only along functional lines. In both these mutually complementary forms of explanation these rights emerge as weapons in a battle which in reality is waged around other orders than those at issue in drawing up the programme of human rights. The sociological explanation also clearly shows why the proclamation of human rights could have reached such heights of pathos: it was in fact formulating a specific, economic individual interest as a supra-historical general interest. This does not mean, of course, that it is completely consumed by economic interest. Here, too, as with every legitimation of interest, there is an ideological surplus that develops its own dynamic.

As has been shown, human rights universalism was used by the West as a political weapon against communism during the Cold War – long term and with compelling success. With the end of the Cold War its political function has by no means exhausted itself; on the contrary, one can expect its significance to grow even further. Indeed, it has in the meantime developed into the ethical framework of a new world order which, on the one hand, ideologically supports the hegemonic order resulting from the victory of the West in the Cold War, and, on the other, de-legitimised the colonial dependencies and helped the peoples of the so-called "Third World", the "third estate" of global society who attained their political independence in the course of de-colonisation, to a formal equality of rights and a new self-awareness. They all made use of the language of human rights morally to justify their claim to liberation from colonial dependence and to a political partnership based on equal rights as part of the newly emergent economic global society. Thus human rights became the common ethical basis of understanding for global political exchange to whose principles tribute has to be paid at least in rhetoric word, with utterly contradictory consequences in deed. The abstract universal avowal of human rights calls for their specific interpretation in concrete situations, which necessarily means that existential contradictions in interest must be articulated in the universalistic language of human rights and must conflict.

For if the universality of ethics depends on the emergence of a global society, the latter will be burdened with the same contradictions and tensions as the former already is. World-wide recognition of the principles of human rights will then not only provide the basis for world-wide understanding but also a common battlefield on which each of the competing sides will wage their battles aimed at asserting their own interests through the appropriate interpretation of the stated principles, to the exclusion of all other interpretations, which for their part are also interest-driven. Together with Panajotis Kondylis, whose analysis I espouse here without reservations, one has to give an emphatic warning about the illusion that the "nominal value" of ideas could prevent their instrumentalisation in polemic. If that were so, wars – as was mentioned earlier – would never have taken place between nations that belonged to the same religion and the same cultural circle, and there should never have been any persecution of heretics or any "purges" in political parties, the "communities of values" *par excellence*.

International law and international organisations have become indispensable in view of the density of today's international traffic, the economic inter-dependence, the instantaneous world-wide communication system and global politics, and it is obvious that they have to be structured according to universal standards of behaviour. As a forum for understanding, however, they also provide the ground for disputes and conflicts. They are their "dispositive", as Michel Foucault would say.

It would, indeed, be an idealistic illusion to believe that the principles of global politics result from the submission of political action to certain norms that are universally recognised; rather, the opposite is true: norms universal in character occur as the idealistic accompaniment to political, social and economic phenomena on a global scale and are intended to regulate traffic between states at least in times that are perceived generally as normal.

Admittedly, extreme situations of self-assertion, such as states of emergency, wars or civil wars, which can also come about through contradictory interpretations of the pathos of the same ethical maxims, are still ex-territorial compared with conventional moral reasoning: there is no war without war crimes, and civil war is always hell precisely because it represents the extreme form of moral commitment; unlike a war between states the enemy is everywhere and seen as a criminal who has to be eliminated – the total destruction of the enemy is in principle the essence of civil war. There is no opportunity for a capitulation to preserve one's identity in exchange for interests. That is why, once one side has won, massacres are always followed by the liquidation, expulsion or "re-education" of the other side. The greatest destruction and suffering in history to date have not been caused by pragmatic politicians, relativists, sceptics or nihilists but by idealists, moralists and normativists.

The taboo on killing is probably as old as the history of civilisation yet the overwhelming majority of organised slaughters was committed in the name of good – except of course that in each case the victims held a different view.

The emergence of global politics spans the whole of modern times; in form it is becoming more and more self-contained and continual, initially through the creation of larger spheres of influence, then later, after the age of discovery in the 16th century, during the establishment of the colonial system and the world market in the 17th and 18th centuries. ("World history did not always exist; but history as the result of world history," wrote Karl Marx in a scribbled note.) It achieved its initial fulfilment, albeit with a hierarchical structure in broad outlines only, in the 19th century with the imperialism of the European industrial states. While the colonial partitioning of the world meant that the entire globe had become the political sphere of action for the European powers, there could not for this reason be any talk of global ethics.

Despite the popularity of imperialism even among the proletariat of the colonial powers, it remained a middle-class liberal undertaking in terms of both its driving force and its organisation. In the 19th century this was apparent not least in the parallelism between the inner structure of the liberal capitalistic states and the structure of the imperialistic world system as a whole: the segregation or relationship between middle-class citizen and proletarian in the former was mirrored in the segregation or relationship between the ruling and the colonial peoples in the latter. The ideological trim accompanying imperialism was a pseudo-scientific racial theory and a Euro-centric ethnology that sanctioned the hierarchical structure of the global balance of power through a value hierarchy of peoples and nations.

It took two world wars, the Russian Revolution and above all the creation and spread of industrial mass production to do away with this situation of a morally sanctioned hierarchy within the global system and to establish a situation of formal equality of status both between nations and between citizens within individual states. The weakening of the empires due to the wars and the ensuing system rivalry favoured the struggle for independence in the colonies, which then resulted in a vast emergence of new nations and states established on an equal legal footing. Within advanced industrial societies, however, mass production undermined the oligarchic liberalism to such an extent that the liberal principle of freedom became economically substantiated, mass production enabled and required mass consumerism, and the mass democracy triggered as a result replaced the more or less oligarchic entities of the élite and their rigid hierarchies with a social mobility which was in principle unlimited. The liberal ideology in consumerist mass democracies thus cast off its traditional middle-class characteristics, became inflationary and acquired individualistic, egalitarian, libertarian, hedonistic and at the same time value-pluralistic traits that are alien to classic puritan liberalism. The emergence of a trans-national mass society, informed through networking and driven by the international division of labour and the globalisation of financial capital, enabled the creation of something resembling a global society for the first time in the history of mankind; while it is admittedly characterised by substantial economic inequalities and cultural differences, it does embrace the equality in principle of the fundamental rights of its members. Obviously these rights are less implemented at the international level and in relations between states than they are within the industrially developed mass democracies; nonetheless, they are constantly propagated in the political rhetoric and required by international law.

Racist and culturalist views that were sanctioned by colonialist and imperialist domination and, even up until the First World War, were far more widespread and self-evident among the political and intellectual élite throughout Europe and the United States than one is willing to admit today – the terrible shadow cast by the Shoa in the cultural heart of Europe has obscured the earlier racism in the West – are theoretically de-legitimised and morally disapproved of; they have been replaced on the one hand by universalist anthropological theories and principles of global ethics and, on the other, by a shoulder-patting appreciation of different cultures, their uniqueness and their contribution to universal culture. Conversely, this means that in their life-shaping, i.e. ethically binding, core of truth they are no longer genuinely taken seriously – and are thus reduced to the level of folklore.

In this sense, at least as a legitimising principle and as a rallying cry for the leading élite, "global ethics" are today no longer an illusion; rather, they have become a reality.

An illusion, however, would be to hope for an end to global conflicts as a result of this. For the expectations the West has raised through the global export of its ethical universalism are potentially explosive.

To the extent namely that western consumerism imbues and destroys traditionally frugal cultures, it will also set free in poor countries the material greediness that is constitutive for rich industrial states and vital on pain of crisis. Within the framework of the now global moral commitments such greediness will emerge as ethical demands, i.e. universal human rights will be interpreted and claimed in material terms, which at the international level will necessarily lead to a battle of human rights against human rights.

Conversely, one should not overrate these repercussions of the West's moral exports either; indeed, compared with all pre-industrial modes of production, the struggles for income in the industrial-capitalist world system are not, for the first time in history, zero-sum games. Given a judicious policy, everyone could benefit – admittedly some more than others. What is important here is not so much static fairness in distribution as well-understood dynamic self-interest, what the great military theorist Carl v. Clausewitz called the "tactfulness of judgement".

For all that, international struggles for income will also retain their significance in a global economy – particularly so; on the common battlefield of a universal ethic they will become even tougher. In any case the fact that universal-ethical precepts and human rights in particular are still being – and for the foreseeable future will continue to be – practised, subject to the far-reaching proviso of state sovereignty, may be interpreted as a precautionary measure to keep their explosiveness under political control. In actual fact this is a contradiction, yet actually submitting state foreign policy activities to universal-ethical principles would destroy the notion of statehood as it would criminalise the reason of state as a legitimate guideline for state action and, in doing so, strip the state of its sovereignty.

The reason there is a contradiction between ethical universalism and a state-like form of organisation for a nation's peoples is that the natural-law justification of human rights stipulates that all human beings possess elementary legal titles that precede all political forms of organisation and the development of genuine legal relationships. If, however, legal titles are not to remain pure fiction, they require a power of sanction, otherwise serious talk of rights is impossible. As the most important political thinker of our early modern times, Thomas Hobbes, once said: "Auctoritas, non veritas facet legem". It is foreseeable that this contradiction between international state law and universalistic individual law will not only keep the international law debate on tenterhooks in the future but also stake out the lines of conflict along which the real political debate will take place.

In spite of all international law concerns, an increase in

military interventions by the West in order to enforce human rights in other parts of the world is to be expected in the future. Indeed, in a consumer culture sentimentalised through the mass media, legality ranks below legitimacy every time, and legitimacy is easily achieved: all it takes is a channelled provocation of the general public. Although this provocation can easily get out of control as a result of emancipated media power, and it can irritate or distract, establish or even prevent rational interest-driven intervention measu-res, the choice of intervention objectives is generally made according to geopolitical considerations. This means, how-ever, that human rights universalism will not be able to develop on an abstract and general plane, at its "nominal value" and independently of the nature of its representatives and addressees. It will have to do so according to those players who wield the power of interpretation and the power of sanction, players who will instrumentalise it. If, however, universalism is instrumentalised and made to serve the purposes of state, it ipso facto becomes particularised, i.e. undermined from within. The concrete and necessarily selective enforcement of abstract and universal principles, whether through military force or economic sanctions, would mean a weakening of the sovereign statehood of one side and at the same time result in the strengthening of that of the other. The consequence would be a selective dissolution of state sovereignty through the interventions of hegemonic powers who would legitimise themselves by invoking human rights; in other words, not an egalitarian ethical universalism but a universally ethically legitimised hegemonic order – a "human rights imperialism," as Samuel Huntington has called this new world order[4]. The fact that these contradictory forces use the same vocabulary, only with a different syntax, constitutes the universality of the ethical phenomenon.

IV.

A global ethic based on human rights universalism is the ideal complement to the globalisation of mass democratic phenomena as a result of the industrial capitalist world system. Its world-wide implementation would not mean the end of conflicts but the creation of a common ground – for understanding as well as for battles.

As long as human beings worthy of the name exist, they will go on arguing about what is good and what is evil in any given situation – irrespective of whether they do so on a common "basis of values". They will also fight for their convictions, to the death if need be. Even if human beings were ever to become sisters and brothers, nothing would change in this regard: after all, the Atrides were also one big family.

In a conversation with Eutyphron, Plato cites Socrates as saying:

"What, then, would we have to quarrel about, what sort of a decision would we be unable to reach in order to argue with one another and become enemies? Let me state it and consider whether it might be this: the fair and the unfair, the noble and the bad, the good and the evil. Are these not, then, the matters over which we will become enemies whenever we do, as we argue and find ourselves

---

[4] S. Huntingdon, op. cit., page 41

unable to reach a full decision, you and I as well as the rest of mankind?"

I cannot see how this could ever change.

International Law Versus the Rights of Man?

HANSPETER NEUHOLD

1. The General Political Background

Standards of international law can be understood as standards which give practical expression to the value concepts of those who are subject to international law, principally states. As in the past, these value concepts continue to set the tone for international relations, much as some observers are surprised by this. In particular, these values provide the criteria for achieving a balance of opposing interests, which is repeatedly the objective of even international law. "Classical international law", which arose out of the development of the modern territory-based state system following the 1648 Treaty of Westphalia which marked the end of the Thirty Years' War, was operated over centuries by European "western" states. On the basis of superiority in all relevant areas of life, ranging from military potential through technological advancement in other disciplines to the state organisation itself, their predominant power enabled the western states to treat the rest of the world as inferiors and to establish dependent colonial relationships outside Europe.

The common platform of values of these western states, strengthened from the end of the 18th century by the emergence of the USA especially, was only fundamentally called into question following the 1917 October Revolution in Russia. Advocates of communist ideology, espoused following the Second World War in numerous states in Eastern

Europe and on other continents, believed that in fact there were unbridgeable contradictions between their own economic and social models and those of the western capitalist countries. Moreover, the common basis of values of the global international system was further challenged by the new states in the "Third World" which achieved independence in the wake of de-colonisation after 1945. Their political alignment was determined by the backwardness of their economic development in comparison with the industrialised countries, and by their own particular political concerns, as well as by cultural traditions which differed from those in the west.

With the collapse of the communist system in Eastern Europe, and the end of the east-west conflict which resulted from it, one of the ideological polarisations fell away, arguably the polarisation which was most wide-spread and the most far-reaching in its consequences. The remaining communist regimes, e.g. in Cuba or Vietnam, are of little consequence if viewed on the global scale. Admittedly, in this respect there is one important exception: China, given its mix of communist ideology with elements of liberal market economy on the one hand, and the status of a developing country with superpower aspirations on the other, together with the continuing presence of Confucian traditions, is assuming a special position which is difficult to classify and constantly changing. However, in general terms there has been a strengthening of the platform of universal ethical principles, and of their reinforcement into international law, since the political changes which began in 1989. This has come about as the post-communist reform countries in the former Soviet bloc and in the former Yugoslavia have dedicated themselves to the western values of pluralist democracy, of human rights oriented towards the individual, of the rule of law and of the market economy.

2. Positive Developments in the Recent Past

Against this background, a number of developments in international law can be identified which have fundamental consequences and which can be viewed positively in terms of global ethics.

Firstly, over the past decades universal provisions relating to the community of states have been carried through and strengthened into international law – principally standards relating to peremptory rights *(ius cogens)* and thereafter the concepts of *erga omnes* obligations and of international crimes of state; these areas are largely covered by international law, and inevitably so, given the material scope included in such law.

As early as 1969, *ius cogens* was bindingly embedded in the Vienna Convention on the Law of Treaties, at least insofar as it relates to the parties to any particular treaty. Under Article 53 of this Convention, treaties which violate peremptory rights under international law are invalid[5]. This means that even sovereign states are not free to conclude treaties on any matter they choose. Their freedom to conclude treaties under international law is limited by

---

[5] Jerzy Sztucki, Ius Cogens and the Vienna Convention on the Law of Treaties: A Critical Appraisal, Österreichische Zeitschrift für öffentliches Recht, Supplementum No. 3 (1974); Giorgio Gaja, "Ius Cogens" beyond the Vienna Convention, Recueil des cours de l'Académie de droit international 172 (1981), pp.275-313; Stefan Kadelbach, Zwingendes Völkerrecht *(Peremptory Rights under International Law)* (1992); Lauri Hannikainen, Peremptory Norms (Ius Cogens) in International Law (1988).

boundaries marking where such treaties go against the higher values of the community of states which are at the root of peremptory right. However, the vital question as to which standards under international law should actually be accorded this higher status remains unanswered in the Vienna Convention. Such provision as exists in the Convention offers little assistance over this question: under Article 53, the general description of *ius cogens* states that a peremptory standard is accepted and recognised by the international community of states as a whole to be a standard from which states cannot deviate, and which can only be changed through a subsequent standard of the same legal standing. Moreover, the system contained in the Vienna Convention only allows for parties to a treaty to assert that the treaty is invalid. It would seem highly unlikely that a state which had concluded a treaty which violated peremptory rights would have such a change of mind. It should also be pointed out that the main significance of the conditions of the Vienna Convention lies in setting out the fundamental direction to be taken in repect of *ius cogens*, and not in elaborating on the everyday pratice of treaty rights, where offences against *ius cogens* play practically no part.

This deficiency is made good by the concept of *erga omnes* obligations[6]. In a definition which has subsequently been repeatedly quoted, the International Court of Justice (ICJ) paraphrased these obligations in the 1970 Barcelona

---

[6] Jochen A Frowin, Die Verpflichtungen erga omnes im Völkerrecht und ihre Durchsetzung *(Erga omnes Obligations in International Law, and their Implementation)* in: Rudolf Bernhardt et al. (Editors), Völkerrecht als Rechtsordnung – Internationale Gerichtsbarkeit – Menschenrechte *(International Law as Legal Order – International Jurisdiction – Human Rights)*, Festschrift for Hermann Mosler (1983), pp. 241-262; Claudia Annacker, The Legal

Traction case as standards which are of importance to all states, so that all states have a legal interest in their observance[7]. As examples, the Court cited the prohibition of aggression and of genocide, but also fundamental human rights including protection against slavery and racial discrimination. Violations of *erga omnes* obligations in international law can therefore not only be asserted by the subject who is directly affected by it, but by all parties – or in the case of a multilateral treaty, by all parties to the treaty. Some matters remain unanswered, such as the question of whether all parties entitled to make a claim must make common cause or whether individual states can act alone in instances where there is a violation of an *erga omnes* obligation and where, for example, there is a demand for compensation or where counter-measures are being initiated. If common cause is required, then offenders would often be able to get away without suffering negative consequences, and if individual states can act independently then differences of opinion and different reactions can be expected. In addition, there are no generally accepted criteria for *erga omnes* standards and no generally accepted catalogue of such standards exists.

In this respect, progress has been made in that "international crimes of state" have been incorporated into the draft Article of the International Law Commission of the United Nations concerning state responsibility[8]. This third aspect

---

Regime of erga omnes Obligations in International Law, Austrian Journal of Public and International Law 46 (1994), pp. 131-166; Bruno Simma, From Bilateralism to Community Interest in International Law, Recueil des cours de l'Académie de droit international 250 (1994), pp. 229-384.

[7] I.C.J. Reports 1970, pp. 3-52.

of matters of general concern to the community of states was paraphrased by the Commission as being a violation of an international obligation, an obligation so essential for the protection of the fundamental interests of the international community that the breaking of that obligation is recognised as a crime by the community as a whole. The International Law Commission (ILC) added a non-exhaustive list of international crimes to this statement, encompassing grave violations in the following areas:-

– against world peace and international security, such as through aggression against another state;

– against the right of peoples to self-determination, for example through enforced colonial rule;

– against fundamental human rights, e.g. through acts of slavery, genocide or apartheid;

– against principles of international environmental law, such as through massive pollution of the atmosphere or of the seas.

International crimes of state should, in the opinion of the Commission, entail particular measures taken against the violating state which go beyond those used to punish "normal" violations of international law. In particular, the Commission puts forward the view that when an international crime of state is committed, all other states should be con-

---

[8] Pierre-Marie Dupuy, Observations sur le crime international de l'Etat (Observations on International Crimes of State), Revue générale de droit international public 84 (1980), pp. 449-486; Joseph H.H. Weiler/Antonio Cassese/Marina Spinedi (Editors), International Crimes of State: A Critical Analysis of the ILC's Draft Article 19 on State Responsibility (1989); Robert Rosenstock, Crimes of States – an Essay, in: Konrad Ginther et al. (Editors), Völkerrecht zwischen normativem Anspruch und politischer Realität (International Law between normative aspirations and political reality). Festschrift for Karl Zemanek on the occasion of his 65th birthday (1994), pp. 319-334.

sidered as "injured states". The ILC's draft Article proposes that on the one hand other states should not formally recognise the situation created as a result of the crime and should not support the offending state in maintaining this situation. On the other hand, they must co-operate with other states in fulfilling these obligations and over measures to resolve the situation brought about by the criminal action. Beyond this, the injured states are entitled to claim compensation and can adopt counter-measures.

The final version of the ILC draft Article on State Responsibility, particularly with the definitive inclusion of international crimes of state as part of the draft, is still awaited. A further unanswered question is whether this draft proposal will be transformed into a treaty on international law, or whether it is to be adopted in a less binding form.

For the argument put forward in this essay, the essential feature is that community aspects have been developed in various fields of international law, even if in part there are only signs of the start of such a process. The areas of standards covered by *ius cogens*, *erga omnes* obligations and international crimes of state largely overlap, with the *erga omnes* concept being considered as the most extensive in scope and that of international crimes of state the most narrowly defined.

It is no matter of chance that the central elements of this development are a ban on the use of aggression, fundamental human rights and the most important principles of international environmental law. In all three areas, the common element is the desire to avert threats to human existence. In the event of war, large numbers of human lives would be lost at one time, and if nuclear weapons were used then all of humanity might be wiped out under some circumstances. Massive violations of human rights can similarly have the same consequences through acts of genocide, or can lead to living conditions which are unworthy of humans, such as through slavery or race discrimination. Where environmental destruction is concerned, the existence of future generations is also principally at risk. From the viewpoint of global ethics, it is to be welcomed that these standards of international law are being given a special legal status which in particular should increase the penalty for violating them.

A second positive development worthy of mention concerns greater respect for human rights, going beyond the points just mentioned. Most recently, less progress has been made in the area of extending the inventory of rights which all human beings should enjoy, although additional protection is imperative particularly as a result of technological developments, e.g. in the fields of information technology and in genetics. Nevertheless, with the exception of these gaps, the three "generations" of human rights already largely take sufficient account of the need to offer guarantees of protection, in terms of content: the "first generation" of civil and political rights, which originated in the west, addresses physical integrity and freedom of the individual, together with the individual's participation in political life; the "second generation" addresses economic, social and cultural rights and is mainly arranged in response to collective needs; and the "third generation" of human rights, which is mainly driven by the developing countries, aims to address the needs of peoples rather than individuals, e.g. over the right to development. Clearly, this last category of rights is underpinned by the understandable concerns of developing countries, yet it contradicts the traditional understanding of human rights as individual rights and presents particular difficulties when it comes to realising and implementing these rights.

However welcome the triumph of the western model of society may be in many respects, we should not overlook the fact that neglecting the social dimension, and, with it, "second generation" human rights, could lead to a situation where we see a spirited revival of Marxist demands rather than the predicted "end of history"[9]. This could well be the case if there is mass poverty or mass unemployment.

In terms of a global ethic, it should be noted that human rights have been embedded in a variety of globally negotiated treaties which are binding under international law, under the auspices of the United Nations. Firstly, mention should be made of the "bundles" of rights in the two United Nations' Covenants agreed in 1966, covering Economic, Social and Cultural Rights (Covenant I) and Civil and Political Rights (Covenant II). These covenants were agreed once generally outlined human rights, as contained in the United Nations' Charter, were given specific definition in the Universal Declaration of Human Rights passed in 1948 in Resolution 217 (III) of the United Nations' General Assembly[10]. Secondly, separate conventions have been passed in response to the need to offer particular protection to certain categories of people, such as women and children, or to act against particularly abhorrent violations of human rights such as genocide and torture.

Despite some legal moves in this direction, we are still awaiting effective assertion of individual human rights

---

[9] Francis Fukuyama, The End of History and the Last Man (1992).
[10] This Declaration, as a resolution passed by the UN General Assembly, is not binding under international law, despite its massive political importance.

against a violating state, and also especially against one's own state, by the individual concerned. A notable breakthrough in this area has been achieved with the entry into force of Additional Protocol XI to the European Convention on Human Rights, in the regional context of the Council of Europe. From now on, on the basis of this Convention and the additional protocols attached to it, protected persons can themselves raise claims of violations of human rights before a permanent court, the European Court of Justice for Human Rights, whose decisions are binding upon those states found guilty of committing violations. This practical step is a further advance along the way. Whereas under "classical" international law the treatment of a state's own citizens was left to the state itself, today the individual has achieved the status of being acknowledged under international law as the bearer of human rights, and has entered the international stage as an independent player. In Europe, individuals can also lay claim to these rights before an independent court, thereby putting themselves on an equal legal footing with sovereign states, as far as human rights are concerned.

Meanwhile it has been generally recognised that human rights have universal validity and no longer number amongst the purely internal affairs of states; instead, the promotion and guaranteeing of human rights represent legitimate concerns for the international community. This was made particularly clear in the closing document of the 1993 UN World Conference on Human Rights in Vienna[11].

---

[11] Text in: Österreichische außenpolitische Dokumentation. Sondernummer "Österreichische Außenpolitik 1993: Schwerpunkt Menschenrechte" *(Documentation on Austrian Foreign Policy. Special issue "Austrian Foreign Policy 1993: Focus on Human Rights")* (1993) pp. 136-169.

In practical terms, an important positive role in asserting human rights is played by the media and by international non-governmental organisations, such as Amnesty International, which can exert effective pressure on state governments.

Therefore it is not only practical constraints of an objective material nature which are constantly further eroding state sovereignty, defined as independence and equality in foreign affairs and autonomy in internal affairs. In an era of globalisation brought about above all by progress in the areas of information handling and transport, the state can perform its duties less and less exclusively within its own borders, and international relations between a superpower and "micro-states" at different ends of the political spectrum are increasingly strongly marked by a de facto inequality and asymmetrical interdependence. In addition to this, political-ideological developments also cut across sovereignty and call into question the concept of the all-powerful state as a higher authority to which the individual citizen must subordinate him- or herself.

A third development worthy of mention in the present context is the start of moves to overcome the principle of collective responsibility under international law, which is questionable from an ethical perspective. Under that principle, measures taken against the violating state affect the entire population of a state and not specifically those people who decided to commit a breach of international law and then carried it out. Indeed, the effects of measures such as economic sanctions cause the "little people" in the violating state to suffer, not their political elite. Sometimes attempts are made to justify this unsatisfactory situation using the argument that the people being affected in this way could always elect to have a leadership which acts in a way which respects international law – this is often a cynical illusion, when considering totalitarian dictatorships with their police apparatus and army units loyal to the regime, on account of the privileges which they enjoy under that regime.

After the "prologue" represented by the war crimes tribunals of Nuremberg and Tokyo following the Second World War, which seemed for a long time to be an isolated instance of justice dispensed by the victorious side, a first act in the drama of global ethics did ultimately follow several decades later, in the early 1990s. However, the jurisdiction of the tribunals set up by the UN Security Council to sentence those people responsible for grave violations of humanitarian law in the former Yugoslavia and in Rwanda was not only restricted to consideration of particularly serious criminal acts, but was also geographically and temporally restricted to specific conflicts.

For that reason, the acceptance in 1998 of the Statute of the International Criminal Court at a conference of states under the auspices of the United Nations in Rome represented a milestone, all the more so since many observers did not expect it to happen[12]. It specifies that this court will possess a general jurisdiction over genocide and grave violations against the articles of war and international humanitarian law. Not only will those contracting states whose members have committed one of the criminal acts named in the statute be subject to its authority, but also those states on whose territory the criminal acts were committed. Additionally, the Statute of the International Criminal Court con-

---

[12] Mahnoush H. Arsanjani, The Rome Statute of the International Criminal Court, American Journal of International Law 93 (1999), pp. 22-43.

tains an express provision, similar to the statutes of the tribunals at The Hague and Arusha, that an official position held by the accused, including that of head of state or government, neither exonerates the accused from prosecution nor represents grounds for lenient treatment.

3. Negative Trends

All these positive improvements should, however, not obscure the fact that deficiencies continue to exist and that there are unwelcome events and trends. The community provisions contained in international law still largely exist only on the printed page, and there is a need for further explanation of important details. Even with the most firmly legally established element, *ius cogens*, there is yet to be a case to serve as a precedent which might set out the direction of future development; such a case will occur when a treaty is declared invalid on grounds of violation of peremptory rights under international law, specifically through the agency of the responsible International Criminal Court in accordance with the Vienna Convention on the Law of Treaties.

In contrast to the end of the secular east-west conflict and the globalisation of human rights, there is an increase in conflicts which are founded on religious or social-philosophical beliefs and the concepts of human rights which derive from them and which differ from western conceptions. This applies particularly to Islamic belief, with its customs of criminal punishment which are archaic and inhuman (e.g. the stoning of adulterers or the surgical removal of the hand of a thief) and its discrimination against certain groups of people (particularly women)[13]. Confucian models of society, hierarchically constructed and oriented along collectivist lines, differ markedly from western concepts in some respects. These contrasts found expression in defeats under international law as reservations were introduced regarding human rights treaties; under these reservations, Islamic states declared the precedence of Sharia law, that is to say Islamic law or state law which is oriented along Islamic principles[14]. In doing so, the question of the legal effect of such reservations is raised and requires clarification, although western states regard them as inadmissible since they are incompatible with the aims and objectives of the treaties. The theory put forward by Samuel Huntington about the "clash of civilisations" being the future global conflict which overshadows all other differences is surely wide of the mark. But it would be equally wrong to ignore the danger which religious fundamentalism in particular represents[15].

Lamentably, the extension of human rights protection through instruments of international law is only partially

---

[13] Heiner Bielefeldt, Menschenrechte und Menschenrechtsverständnis im Islam *(Human rights and the conception of human rights in Islam)*, Europäische Grundrechte Zeitschrift 17 (1990), pp. 489-498; Bassam Tibi, Im Schatten Allahs. Der Islam und die Menschenrechte *(In the Shadow of Allah: Islam and human rights) (1994)*; Ann Elisabeth Mayer, Islam and Human Rights: Traditions and Politics (1995).

[14] On this general issue, and other areas, Lilly Sucharipa-Behrmann, The Legal Effects of Reservations to Multilateral Treaties, Austrian Review of International and European Law 1 (1996), pp. 67-88; see also Bruno Simma, Reservations to Human Rights Treaties – Some Recent Developments in: Gerhard Hafner/Gerhard Loibl/Alfred Rest/ Lilly Sucharipa-Behrmann/Karl Zemanek (editors), Liber Amicorum. Festschrift for the 80th birthday of Ignaz Seidl-Hohenveldern (1998), pp. 659-682.

[15] Samuel Huntington, The Clash of Civilizations and the Remaking of World Order (1997).

realised in practice. One only needs to cast a glance over the reports produced by Amnesty International to establish that massive violations of even the most fundamental human rights still continue to take place in many states as a matter of routine.

The International Criminal Court can only begin its work once 60 states have become party to its statute. It is currently still difficult to estimate when this might take place. Moreover, the jurisdiction of the Court is limited to those states which are party to the statute. From this it can be assumed that this treaty will not be ratified by precisely those states which might have to reckon with proceedings against its citizens in the Court. Moreover, even in its dealings with those states which are party to its statute, the Court will be dependent on the readiness of those states to fulfil their obligation to co-operate with the Court.

"Operation Allied Force", which was conducted by NATO against the Federal Republic of Yugoslavia and was intended mainly to prevent a humanitarian disaster in Kosovo, threw up a further dilemma for international law: key principles of international law can come into conflict with one another, even principles which can be considered part of *ius cogens*, deemed to have an *erga omnes* effect, and violation of which would be considered as an international crime of state and ought to result in particular measures being taken against the violating state. In the example mentioned, there was a clash between the ban on the use of force and the protection of fundamental human rights. Opinions were divided over which principle should be given precedence at the expense of the other. The author of this essay was amongst those who consider the air attacks carried out by member states of NATO against Yugoslavia to be contrary to international law, because they were not covered by either of the two exceptions to the ban on the use of force contained in Article 2, paragraph 4 of the United Nations' Charter[16]. NATO states were not acting to exercise their right to collective self-defence, as no armed attack had been carried out against any member of the alliance; nor had the UN Security Council issued an authority to use force under the framework of the system for collective security, in accordance with Chapter VII of the UN Charter. Looking beyond the laws contained in the UN Charter, there is still no adequate legal basis for "humanitarian intervention", and specifically there is no justification for it in common international law. This is not to say that "Operation Allied Force" cannot be considered to have been politically defensible, indeed even a political necessity. There are exceptional situations where other values take precedence over the observance of the law as currently constituted. Moreover, this holds true not just for the incomplete "primitive" international law. This much, at least, can be agreed by all those who do not see the law as an end in itself, but principally as a means of social control.

---

[16] Similarly, amongst others, Bruno Simma, NATO, the UN and the Use of Force: Legal Aspects, European Journal of International Law 10, (1999) (no page reference could be given for the magazine as the document was only issued on the internet at the time of writing).

A State as Work In Progress

Hedy Fry

The theme of the meeting *Cultural Pluralism and Global Ethics*, is a timely one. As we approach the dawn of the new century, we realize that within a single generation the world has changed remarkably.

Liberalization of trade and communications technologies has blurred national borders. While this evolution has generated optimism, it has also created anxiety.

The hope that globalization will create "economic benefit for all" and narrow the gap between rich and poor countries is tempered by concerns that the door will be opened to increased exploitation of disadvantaged peoples.

The expectation that the forging of global economic liaisons will enhance understanding and respect for cultural diversity is clouded by fears of homogeneity and assimilation into one dominant global culture.

Yet, and I quote my colleague, Pierre Pettigrew: "globalization seems to me to be capable of serving individuals and their societies if, and only if, it respects the freedom of action of human beings and allows them room to maneuver … The **economy** (the objective of globalization), is **the** arena in which human beings can fulfill themselves – innovate and create – but only if politics, through careful intervention, can keep the market in line and prevent the intolerable inequities that would result from unbridled materialism."

I would like to pursue this theme by referring to the Canadian experience.

Canada today is a global nation. 42% of Canadians claim origins other than English, French or Aboriginal. Among countries of its size, 30 million or larger, Canada has the highest percentage of foreign-born residents – 18%; 12% of whom are new citizens – and we receive 25% of the UNHCR's refugees. Cultural pluralism in Canada is not an option. It is a given.

Cultural pluralism in Canada has an open ended definition. It broadens the traditional definition of culture as art, literature, music to encompass the values of our people. Pluralism reflects the changing nature of our society and has evolved to include more than race, ethnicity and religion, but gender, sexual orientation and disability as well. Currently we are reviewing our Human Rights Act to reflect more accurately the nature of pluralism.

In fact, our country is a product of a process driven by cultural pluralism. In wave after wave for the past 400 years, people from over 100 different cultural and linguistic backgrounds have contributed to the building of the country that is Canada. Many of these people chose Canada. Others simply found themselves on our shores, often supported by nothing other than hope. And they continue to come.

Yet, our record of welcome is not pristine. It has been marred by episodes of intolerance that today haunt and direct our national discourse. Colonialism itself has left on the Aboriginal peoples deep scars that have not yet healed. The internment of Japanese Canadians during the war, the refusal to allow citizenship to Asians as recently as 50 years ago, and the Chinese Head Tax remain as shameful blots on the pages of our history.

Yet, in Canada today, we consider our greatest strength to be the diversity of our people.

Some say that Canada was born out of serendipity – others, that it was out of necessity – the need to create social cohesion in a vast and disparate land with a sparse and diverse population.

Whatever the reason, it was during the process of learning from our past mistakes, of seeking ways to ameliorate their negative effects, that Canadians developed particular skills – skills of compromise, negotiation, accommodation and discourse.

These skills created a dynamism in Canada. Nation building is an experiment in progress. Our society, our institutions, our structures of governance are in a constant state of evolution. In order to achieve economic and social stability, we strive always to find balance. As my colleague Pierre Pettigrew puts it: "In Canada there has never been a lasting status quo. Each new generation has had to reinvent the country."

Indeed some may argue that governments in Canada have often been one step behind the will and vision of the people – who have expected us to implement their values in legislation and public policy – and that in turn, this expectation has led to the tradition of careful political intervention by the state, and to partnerships between government and communities in order to manage change. The academics call this engaging civil society – Canadians call it good governance.

In fact, this tendency to political discourse has, as some jokingly put it, become a Canadian cultural trait. It is often said that we create public task forces and Royal Commissions in response to any controversial question – these have been known to last for years.

I guess that's why we are seen as a bland, plodding people.

But in truth, while we engage in discourse region to region, government to people, community to community – we are learning from one another. We see new perspectives, hear wide differences of opinion and needs – and in doing so, better understanding occurs, negotiation proceeds, common ground is found, compromise is achieved – and public policy is formulated – societal evolution occurs.

Over the years, through this process, Canadians have developed a pragmatism that in turn has led to, as some might say, the uninspiring ethic of *peace order and good government*. An ethic that has historically guided political governance and institutional change, that has been sustained by close observation of the rule of law, and that has found life in the pragmatic yet paradoxical solutions – which informs evolving social and economic policy.

In fact, from the beginning, the concept of an integrated society versus the assimilative one adopted by our neighbor to the south, was a politically pragmatic decision.

The two colonial powers found it necessary to peaceful coexistence to acknowledge the distinctiveness of each other's cultures. So Quebec maintained its own language, culture and Napoleonic code of law. Today, most Canadians believe that Quebec's distinctiveness is an essential part of being Canadian.

The arrival of immigrants – from all corners of the globe – created new tensions that challenged the existing definition of cultural pluralism. And in 1971, after a Royal Commission on Bilingualism and Biculturalism heard from a very diverse population – a new paradoxical but pragmatic principle came into being – that of official bilingualism and multiculturalism. One people, two languages, many cultures bound together by the ethics of tolerance, respect for differences and a common bond of citizenship.

Some have referred to today's Canada as a post-modern global state. In fact, it was a Canadian, Marshall MacLuhan, who predicted the notion of a global village.

Is Canada a global nation? If global means vast expanses of land mass with extraordinary regional disparities – then we are global. If global means a diversity of people representing all of the world's religions, races and cultures – then we are global.

If so, how does the Canadian experience relate to this conference on *Globality and Global Ethics – Myth or Reality*?

Our experiences are our reality. One of the main challenges to globalization is cultural pluralism.

Is it possible to maintain cultural identity in a pluralistic world?

Is it possible to develop a code of social ethics in an economically motivated, market driven world?

Is it possible to foster diversity in a world of mass communication technology that some fear could promote homogeneity?

In Canada we have found these to be possible. And while we do not share the long and complex history of Europe, we are a pluralistic society. Within a framework of ethical governance and common principles we have relied on an integrative model to maintain a diversity of cultural identities. At the same time, we have achieved social cohesion through citizenship and shared values of mutual respect, social responsibility, fairness and accommodation.

Interestingly, we have found that this strengthened a sense of identity and belonging amongst all citizens.

Some among you will point to the movement in Quebec, by sovereignists who seek to create a new nation state and while this is true .... there are no tanks, barbed wire and guns separating Quebec from the rest of Canada.

The separatist party occupies a formal place in the House of Commons and we engage in debate, we wag, shake our fingers at each other – in anger sometimes – but we do so within a civil construct of constitutional argument and adherence to the rule of law.

In fact, the principles of good governance and engagement of civil society continue to guide the evolution of Canadian society.

A legislative framework under the umbrella of the Charter of Rights and Freedoms has evolved over the years to include the Canadian Human Rights Act, Employment Equity Act, the Citizenship Act, the Immigration Act and the Multiculturalism Act which form, if I may be so presumptuous as to say, an ethical mission statement that guides the development of economic and social policies.

However, through experience we have learned in Canada that legislation alone does not guarantee equality or societal change unless supplemented by good public policy and institutional change.

Government undertakes through programs and policies to take strategic steps to ensure that these occur. For example, if we are to encourage a society in which all citizens can participate equally in the political, social, economic and cultural life of a country, institutions must not only reflect the demographics of the population, but must foster an environment that welcomes them.

Let me illustrate. Our Charter of Rights guarantees religious freedom. When orthodox Sikhs wished to join the Royal Canadian Mounted Police, their religion required that they wear at all times, the turban and the kirpan, while the RCMP uniform had a different specific head-gear. After much heated public debate and legal challenges, the Supreme Court ruled that indeed the concept of religious freedoms extends to more than where or how you worship.

Other institutional changes followed. So that now Muslim women in the Armed Forces have been able to wear a modified version of the hijab as part of their uniform

In the same way, community policing models, community sensitivity training and outreach to specific cultural communities, recognizes the fact that some immigrants and refugees bring with them in historical mistrust and fear of police institutions.

In fact, in Canada we have learned that in a culturally diverse society (one could substitute global), government must not only take steps to ensure the equal rights of all its citizens *de jure*, but also *de facto*.

Adopting the principles of civic participation is key to the building of an integrative society ... where citizenship brings certain rights as well as responsibilities; where a sense of belonging is enhanced by being part of the decision-making process; and equality is **NOT** synonymous with sameness, but is flexible enough to make accommodation for difference.

I am an immigrant to Canada. While 18% of us sit in the House of Commons – we are only 12 % of the population. In the early years of nation building, Canada rejected the concept of many nation states in favor of federalism. In keeping with the paradoxical solutions we have found that this facilitated the autonomy of provinces within an overall national structure for citizenship. So that a Canadian in Prince Edward Island or Quebec can enjoy the same social and economic status as in British Columbia.

It has not been an easy task. It requires constant negotiation and political good will – and our indigenous people are still seeking autonomy and self government. Recently, a new territory was formed. Nunavut has a different system of government. One based on consensus (in keeping with aboriginal tradition), and all official business is conducted in Inuktitut, the language of the Inuit people.

We cannot predict the result of this new experiment in the evolution of our federation, but all Canadians watch with pride. We have learned nothing is as constant as change.

I do not offer the Canadian experience to you as a solution to global ethics, nor am I presumptuous enough to believe that Canada is a model for managing a culturally pluralistic society.

Many things are possible.

If we are willing to give up the status quo and embrace change and evolution, anything is possible.

If we put people first, recognizing – that people are the engines of productivity and economic growth – and we are prepared to throw away the artificial barriers that currently divide social and economic policy and accept that they are interdependent. If we are willing to embrace differences, to see in diversity the strength of the human species, and in learning to do so develop the overarching ethos that human rights and concepts of citizenship are the truly unifying forces of globalization.

I hope that as a result of this conference we will find that will.

Nation State – Nation of State – National Minority

ARNOLD SUPPAN

The political "turning point" in the years 1989/1991 led in eastern and south-eastern Europe to the formation of new nation states. Aside from the members of the respective "titular nation", they are naturally also inhabited by members of numerous other nationalities and smaller minorities. In fact, of the some 400 million people living in the eastern half of Europe today (including Turkey), some 50 million are designated as national minorities. Unlike the break-up of the Soviet Union, which to the great surprise of most experts, was amazingly peaceful, the dissolution of Yugoslavia unleashed a veritable chain reaction with wars in Slovenia, Croatia, Bosnia-Herzegovina, Kosovo and Serbia. The main reasons are to be sought less in the mixed national structures than in irresponsible, power-hungry politicians hailing primarily from the "new class" created by Titoism. These leaders displayed no scruples in exploiting nationalistic and religious feelings and in utilising modern mass media and much more than a fraction of the intellectual elite to pit the nations and religious communities of their land against each other. The consequences thus far have been the most devastating in Europe since the Second World War: Mass murder, mass expulsion, mass rape, mass destruction of cultural and economic assets. When the stench of corpses and gun powder finally lifted, it became clear that the new order had serious flaws: What states would continue existing and where would their borders lie? What nations and nationalities were willing to continue or to begin living side by side? – Before projecting ahead, we must first take a look at the past.

The Ideology of the Nation State

The "People" were equated with the political "nation" and "state" as early as the French Revolution. The nation was defined there as a politically self-aware community of citizens treated equally under the law regardless of their social and economic status, ethnic origin or religious convictions.

Although adopted by the Germans, Italians and Russians in the first half of the 19th century, this French model of the nation state was applicable to neither the Habsburg monarchy nor to the Ottoman Empire. Istanbul retained its millet system organised on the basis of religious confession while Vienna propagated the equality of the nationalities in 1848, although not actually implementing it into constitutional law until 1867. With Article XIX of the Fundamental Laws of 21 December 1867, "Cisleithania" (the half of the Dual Monarchy "on this side of", i.e. on the Austrian side of, the Leitha River) became an anomaly in Europe. No other European state at this time had granted its national groups – which totalled nine in the Austrian half of the monarchy – comparable group rights. Basically, they were guaranteed the equal rights of all languages in local use in schools, administration and public life. By contrast, the "Transleithanian" half of the empire was conceived as a Hungarian nation state, and it granted only limited rights to nationalities.

The minority protection clause in the peace treaties of 1919/20 fell far short of the standard set by the law on nationalities in Cisleithania, as did the treaties on minorities concluded in this same period with Poland, Czechoslovakia, Romania, Yugoslavia and Greece. Most importantly, the Allies – following the French nation state model – failed to anchor group rights in law, fearing the creation of a "state within a state." The prevailing concept of state at the time was quite anti-nationalities, a fact underscored by Belgrade and Bucharest more or less having to be forced to sign agreements on these rights, which were only enforceable before the Council of the League of Nations anyway. The new or greatly enlarged states in eastern central and south-eastern Europe saw themselves as "nation states" in which political power was held exclusively by the "nations of state." In November 1917 Lenin proclaimed the sovereignty of all peoples of Russia and their right to self-determination until creation of their own states, at which time, led of course by the proletariat, they would establish a "voluntary and honourable federation of the peoples of Russia." The situation of minorities was improved as little by this proclamation as by Germany and Italy not having to agree to minority protection provisions (except with regard to Upper Silesia and Fiumes). When Hitler and Stalin began using co-national minorities as pawns in their aggression policy between 1938 and 1940, the entire minority protection system of the League of Nations collapsed. The Munich agreement, the Hitler-Stalin Pact and the Vienna arbitration rulings of 1938 and 1940 destroyed not only the protection system for minorities but even more importantly, the new division of nation states created in 1919/20. However, this post World War One order had been little more ethnically homogeneous than the dismantled empires of the Habsburgs, Ottomans and Romanovs. The build-up of a centralised state apparatus on the French model met with vehement opposition on the part of the new national minorities – but also the alleged "nations of state" such as the Slovaks and Croats. Be that as it may, National Socialist Germany and the communist Soviet Union resumed their efforts in 1938/39 to create a new order once again declared as "ethnic." To this end, this region was suddenly subjected to large-scale resettlement programs, not only for Czechs, Jews, Poles, Balts and Slovenes but also for German minorities from the Soviet centre of power. The Red Army was moved to march into eastern Poland on 17 September 1939 primarily with the backing of Ukrainian and White Russian minorities – and the Western powers accepted this situation. Following the deportation, expulsion and annihilation of most members of the minorities in central and eastern Europe during the devastating war between the German Reich and the Soviet Union, Stalin became the man in 1945 who dictated not only the new state and national order of eastern central and south-eastern Europe but its regional minority policies as well. Border shifts favouring the Soviet Union, Poland and Yugoslavia altered majority-minority ratios throughout the region. Most crucially, however, the protection of minorities was henceforth to be supplanted by proletarian internationalism and the forced development of centralised nation states. Belief in this one-sided social identity for each individual relegated the minorities issue to a matter time would solve. Yugoslavia was the only country to constitutionally recognise a number of nationalities apart from the nations forming the state. The question thus arises: Did the Yugoslavian nation state fail as a result of the dictatorial communist system or the decentralisation of the party and the bureaucracy? – The answer is undisputed: Initially as a result of Tito's party and military dictatorship, after 1980 to an increasing extent due to the conflicting interests of the epigones who succeeded him.

On the Tensions Between the State and Society

The history of the eastern part of Europe was shaped well into the 18th century by the repeated influx of immigrants from the West, East and Southeast. This brought together ethnic groups with very different cultural backgrounds in terms of work and everyday life, mores and customs, and with very different cultural experiences. Imagine the mix: German peasants and craftsmen, Jewish, Greek, Aromunic traders, Serb and Romanian livestock breeders and the Ottoman Begs and Agas. During the period of the grand dynastic empires, the coexistence of these diverse ethnic groups from the Baltic states to Macedonia was governed by countless imperial or royal privileges for local, territorial, confessional or personal autonomies. With the Industrial Revolution came new migrations, leading both to further ethnic mixing and to new ethnic concentrations in the large cities that began to form. The bourgeois division of labour encouraged the demise of the old autonomies and the development of large markets for capital, labour, production and trade, yet also demanded an expanded and modern governmental administration that operated if at all possible on the basis of a single official language. The border changes of 1919/20 prevented these capitalistic approaches from being taken, and the new "nation states" made far-reaching changes in the structure of ownership with land reforms and capital transfers, usually at the expense of the national minorities. The greatest beneficiaries were the propertied and educated middle class who belonged to the new "nations of state."

With the National Socialists' "Grossraum" economy, the nation-state borders were once again eliminated and the societies of eastern central and south-eastern Europe were forced to co-operate in German war production, being divided inhumanly in the process into "value categories" based on nation and race. Of course this did not stop the "Greater German Reich" from exploiting 2.5 million Russians and Ukrainians, 900,000 Poles, 230,000 Yugoslavs, 140,000 Czechs, 130,000 Balts, 100,000 Hungarians and 15,000 Greeks as "alien workers" – nor, for that matter, 1.5 million French, 600,000 Italians, 250,000 Belgians, and 230,000 Dutch.

The Soviet program of social equalisation and the destruction of national and religious practices affected the nationalities in a different way after 1945. The collectivisation of agriculture and the socialisation of enterprises, and with it the elimination of private property, destroyed what had formerly been the foundations of societies and their cultures, rendering the individual completely dependent on the state. In the communist social system, there was no longer any room for autonomous spheres. At the same time, several political leaderships sought to introduce a new communist state nationalism while the dominance of Soviet policy incited a new brand of anti-Soviet nationalism. These developments led to strong antipathies toward communist internationalism and strong sympathies for older national ideals, particularly in Poland, Hungary and Rumania. Whereas power changes in 1918 and 1938/39 were unleashed primarily by tensions between state and nation, the transformation in 1989 is largely attributable to the dissolution of the Soviet system, politically, economically and socially. National issues did not begin playing a central role here until a power vacuum was created.

Preconditions for a New Policy on Nationalities

The current European situation opens up for the first time this century the possibility of working towards universal means of regulating nationality and minority problems far removed from great power interests and beyond totalitarian ideologies. A new order in the relations of state and nation, of nation states and national minorities would naturally have to incorporate several basic premises:

a) It must address the global challenges related to security, economics and ecology. Neither a national society nor a homogenised nation state can meet these challenges alone.

b) It must ensure that individuals can develop wherever possible to their fullest potential while being instilled with community identities, be they familial, ethnic, denominational, philosophical, regional or governmental. A conscious national identity in this context is just one of several identities. With increased education, an individual's claim to intellectual and cultural autonomy grows while the all-dominant influence of the state recedes. However, this loosening of ties with the state must not be allowed to lead to a severing of the connections a person has to other "roots."

c) It must expand the nationality problem from strictly legal issues to issues of politics, society, economics and culture. Once passed, laws can only create possibilities, they cannot alter patterns of behaviour in societies.

A new policy on nationalities must also assume the continued existence of nation states. Despite the current trends toward integration, the nation state presumably provides most of its members with a stronger sense of security, belonging and even personal identity than any other larger alternative group can. And the greater the need people have for this type of identity to cope with the pressures and crises of social mobility and alienation from familiar surroundings, the greater remains the potential power of the nation state as a channel for their longings and resistance. The prevailing view today is that the nation state is the most important means of preserving the culture of nations with small populations, for it is the nation state that gives priority to national customs and practices through state school systems and state cultural subsidies. Lastly, the national bureaucracies hold fast to the centralisation of their nation states in their function as organisers of administration and society and along with much of the intelligentsia, view the state as the key institution, one's identity as a citizen of the state as the sole principle for creating community.

The future vision of a new policy on nationalities must

therefore begin by recognising the national diversity of a region and acknowledge this diversity and any religious or cultural diversity as human assets. The nation states must go one step further and safeguard this diversity with all means at their disposal. They can do so by creating political equality for national minorities, by guaranteeing students the right to instruction in their native language regardless of the type of school, and by supporting the national culture of minorities. National views of foreigners, so-called "heterostereotypes", must also be corrected or they will keep poisoning the coexistence of majority and minority. Not least, minorities must be granted social equality of opportunity to prevent the assimilation of the very individuals who are upwardly mobile in society. The essential factor is and remains the creation of a new national awareness that recognises that all national communities living within the territory of a state have contributed to forming it as a societal and cultural entity in the sense of a modern nation. Only this step from nation state to a state of citizens would view "ethnic cleansing" as seriously harmful to the entire society of the state, as self-destructive. The cultural scientist and current Romanian foreign minister, Andrei Plesu, spoke out strongly against all forms of nationalistic hysteria in a 12 June 1999 interview with the *Neue Zürcher Zeitung*: "The crisis in Yugoslavia has proved that nationalism is the fastest way to destroy a nation, particularly nationalism in its most primitive form. I do not believe these barbaric ways of thinking have a chance of survival in the 21st century. In Yugoslavia the spirit of the times fought against the spirit of place, the spirit of the times against the genius loci. The spirit of the times won out. It bid farewell to nationalistic hysteria, to contempt for the individual and his rights, and to a view of sovereignty that permits a state to commit whatever crimes it wishes."

Thoughts on "Globalisation and Gobal Ethics"

Ebenezer Njoh-Mouelle

I shall not attempt here to describe globalisation in all its facets. There is however one aspect of this phenomenon which tends to obscure all the others, namely cyberspace: the new environment in which authors and users of information exchange messages and data via a global network of interconnected computers. Indeed, the words "info-routes" and "information superhighways" are on everyone's lips.

Globalisation, Free Movement... Absolute *laissez faire*?

Globalisation is undoubtedly typified by the free movement of information as well as capital, ideas, goods and individuals beyond national and regional borders. It is a situation in direct contrast with the state of affairs characterised by a relative partitioning of the world; worse still, a policy of closed borders such as was implemented by the China of Mao Tsetung in particular and the entire former East Bloc in general. For these countries closed borders were an everyday reality; they were impervious to western capital, ideas or lifestyles. Indeed, the cinema halls of the East Bloc were closed to western productions just as their theatres rarely played host to troupes or variety and music hall stars from western countries.

This situation inspired the billionaire George Soros, who, in his book "The Trouble with Capitalism"[28], develops a distinction between an "open society" and a "closed society"; while the former refers to the Western Bloc, dominated by economic liberalism, the laws of the market place and democracy, the latter designates the East Bloc, dominated by state planning and dogmatic totalitarianism. With the fall of the Berlin Wall in 1989, closed society suddenly opened up. Even China has opened up to the rest of the world, and one cannot deny the impression that globalisation did indeed take place and acquired its full meaning as of 1989. Even if alongside these two Blocs there was and still is the Third World bloc, there was an opening-up to the East for some and to the West for others. Africa as a whole stood here, for there was neither a closing down (something Africa could ill afford) nor an opening up at all costs. Forced to participate in the mobility of an open society of the capitalist and liberal world through the intermediary of colonisation, Africa has long undergone something of an economic and financial globalisation which has not entirely penetrated its original cultural dimension. I intentionally moderate this judgement, for everyone knows that, at the cultural level also, there is a globalisation or "semi-globalisation" so to speak, expressed through the adoption by Africans of Indo-European languages such as French, English, Spanish, Portuguese or even Italian. Languages specifically designated as languages of wide-scale international communication. It is a "semi-globalisation" nonetheless since alongside these foreign languages Africa still keeps alive many aspects of its

---

[17] George Soros: The Trouble with Capitalism

traditional cultural diversity as well as the overwhelming use of its many languages which, for their part, will have great difficulty in achieving global status.

The Unilateral Nature of "Free Movement"...

While it is pleasing to note that the partitioning of the world's political blocs and cultural regions has today given way to a process of de-partitioning that favours the opening up of nations among themselves, is it true to say that this opening-up is the same for everyone and that all benefit in the same way?

To answer this question we need to examine more closely the concept of free movement, be it of information, ideas, capital and goods, which in short defines the concept of globalisation. It is not necessary to review systematically everything that is in circulation in this way to establish that there is a dissymmetry, not to say an imbalance in this global movement. Let us consider one of them: ideas. Of all the ideas in circulation, those that have every chance of succeeding are those launched from the region in which all the Powers are concentrated; namely the core of the group of the seven most industrialised and wealthiest nations. This is true of the ideas of democracy and human rights. This is true of the idea of "good governance" that can be found in virtually all the speeches by leaders of the countries of the South and in particular the countries of Africa placed under Structural Adjustment. Given that the ideas are those propagated by the circle of leaders of the countries of the northern hemisphere, it is euphemistic to talk of their free movement: they are more or less "directives". And when directives reach you in a balance of power that is utterly unfavourable, you do more than receive them: you execute them. Indeed, when it comes to the free movement of ideas, one needs to consider separately those ideas that originate from private individuals, those who have an e-mail address and who do in fact exchange freely with other correspondents in the world-wide web of interconnected computers. The ideas for action issued by the powerful governments of the world do not necessarily go via the Internet. They are broadcast by radio and television and reach all four corners of the world via satellite aerials. Another manifestation of the revolution in the area of information technologies.

Which of the ideas originating from the countries of the South and the Third World in general have ever managed to circulate successfully around the "global village"? Certain Africans recently sought to disseminate the idea of reparations due to Black people by the slave states during the centuries of the transatlantic slave trade. I hasten to add that I do not personally share this idea; but that is beside the problem I am addressing here. The problem is that the idea itself was not taken up anywhere within the global circuit. It is cloaked in silence, the same silence which for a long time cloaked the despicable practices of the slave trade. The idea stems from the camp of the weak and has no chance whatsoever of making any headway. One should not be deceived into thinking that this is because it is not a good idea. If, however, it had been issued or rather supported by the circle of the great powers of the northern hemisphere, good or bad its circulation would have generated an echo, and there is little doubt that it would have had some sort of effect, in concrete terms. There was a time when the Africa represented in the Organization of African Unity wanted to run an information agency called the P.A.N.A., for Pan African News Agency. It was the expression of a political determination on the part of African governments to add their weight to what they hoped would become the new world order of information. What became of this African struggle? As it did not enjoy the support of the great powers, it failed. The P.A.N.A. failed because it was condemned to fail. It was not an idea of the North!

If I were to take other examples such as capital, services and goods, they would all illustrate abundantly the unilateral nature of the principle of "free movement" as well as the permanent nature of the domination exerted by the law of the strongest.

What of Human Rights When the Law of the Strongest Prevails?

There is no doubt on this subject: the world order continues to be regulated by the law of the strongest. It was already thus in the past, at the time of the supremacy of the Euro-centric approach, which then became the western-centric approach. When people today talk of globalisation, one might be tempted to think that **the globe** is a new idea! At the time of Euro-centric domination everything happened as if the "world and its reality" had huddled up into a single corner of the world, Europe – and that outside Europe the world did not exist. Did not the century of enlightenment cast a shadow over itself by embracing within it the unspeakable official slave trade and slavery itself? While the broad dissemination of anthropological knowledge and the numerous movements aimed at asserting the autonomy and cultural identity of peoples long kept muzzled have contributed to recognising the right to be different, it has hardly altered the balance of power in the world. Viewed from this angle, globalisation, that is to say hegemony, is not a new reality but the deconstruction of an ancient trend that had been expressed through what has been called Euro-centric domination, which today has become western-centric domination.

Against this backdrop stands the problem of the need for a global ethic. True, the novelty does not reside in the rule of the law of the strongest. The novelty that seems to have given rise to recent concerns stems from the *modus operandi* of cyberspace as much as from certain advances in scientific research, particularly genetic modification, which poses a genuine threat to the human genome. To help put some sort of order into cyberspace and the use of the results of scientific and technological research, UNESCO has taken a number of commendable initiatives, to which I shall be referring later.

Before that, I should like to dwell a little on what appears to characterise globalisation at the ethical level, namely the absence of shared values and the continually uncontested supremacy of the law of the strongest, which ultimately is none other than the law of money.

To try and characterise, once again, what is happening within the framework of globalisation, I am tempted to combine what George Soros says about open society and the doctrine of *laissez faire*. In his book mentioned earlier, the Hungarian-born American billionaire writes: "An open society could not exist without shared values. That is why I suggest that open society itself be posited as a fundamental value for which we should make sacrifices. It is more than a system from which we benefit by seeking to satisfy our egotistical yearnings. There is no open society if its members do not consider it as a value per se."[18] By open society Soros is referring to western society, liberal and capitalist, a term which opposed it to the closed society of the communist régimes of the former East Bloc. And within open society, the law of *laissez faire* concerns the market system as such. And here, Soros does not share the opinion of those who believe that the doctrine of *laissez faire* is "self-sufficient", i.e. that markets naturally tend towards equilibrium and do not require any particular efforts to be preserved: "Markets are fundamentally unstable," he says, "contrary to the claims of the ideologists of *laissez faire*, who oppose any form of intervention aimed at restoring a modicum of stability"[19].

Like open society, globalisation can never be a régime of absolute *laissez faire* on the pretext that it is founded on the principle of liberty. Like Kant and Rousseau we know that genuine liberty is one which is capable of submitting itself to law, i.e. to constraint and limitation. And where could such a law come from other than from the determination of states which globalisation does not eliminate. And yet many conventions signed by these states have yet to be ratified by the parliaments of those very states. The convention governing the creation of the International Criminal Court requires sixty signatories to become established and operative. By June 1999 it would seem that only three

---

[18] Soros: op. cit. page 28.
[19] ibid. page 29.

ratifications have been recorded. How should one interpret the fact that for this International Criminal Court, which will hear and determine human rights violations, the great powers themselves do not take the lead to speed up the implementation of this institution, the same powers which trumpet *urbi et orbi* the need to observe those very rights?

Ethical Action Is Not Limited to the Proclamation of Declarations of Principles

And yet I do not see any other way of introducing and ensuring the observance of a minimum of ethical order in the fragmented world we live in today; by this I mean the drawing-up of international conventions on certain issues and the creation of global judicial authorities designed to judge any violations. The United Nations (UN) has already adopted this orientation which consists of getting member states to sign international conventions. But that is not enough. The new, decisive step that is being taken is to implement international jurisdictions. The International Court of Justice at The Hague was set up to hear and determine conflicts between UN member states. Today we need to set up other jurisdictions of the same type as the one based in Arusha to hear crimes against humanity, or the International Criminal Court, which is to pass judgement on human rights violations.

Indeed, there is little point in multiplying solemn declarations, the most recent of which to be issued by UNESCO deal with the protection of the human genome and the safeguarding of future generations. It is important to twin the proclaimed ethical principles with the necessary instruments of coercion without which the most noble declarations of principle would be condemned to remain nothing more than honourable intentions.

The UN Has to be Reformed

Can all this be achieved without a complete reform of the UN? I do not think so. Globalisation has to be an opportunity to reform the UN. This global organisation has to be reformed so that it can assume the great duties of a genuine power, in particular the duties of a peacekeeping and policing force, of a guaranteeing power for the observance of ethical standards and principles approved by all. If it is to move in this direction the UN has to become more democratic and no longer be under the full control of the dynasty of the member states of the Security Council. What I mean is that the Security Council should give way to a Council with a greater number of members, without exceeding one third of the number of member states. The members of this new Council would be democratically elected according to a regional quota to be drawn up according to the population of each electoral group. If one can continue to accept that certain great powers sit permanently on the Council, why should one not reconsider the principle of the right of veto recognised to some?

I do not claim to propose here a reform project for the United Nations. I simply wanted to underscore the idea of the need for such a reform, an ulterior motive being the concern to see the United Nations granted the great and noble mission of ensuring the observance of international conventions and other regulations.

The Need to Introduce an Efficiency Concern in UNESCO's Normative Formulations

As I mentioned earlier, UNESCO, one of the UN's specialist organisations, has already taken a number of good initiatives aimed at contributing some form of regulatory measures for the lack of constraint of globalisation in the field of science and cyberspace. In the field of science one has to applaud the creation of two bodies: the International Bioethics Committee (IBC) and the World Commission on the Ethics of Scientific Knowledge and Technology (COMEST). The IBC is already up and running and its achievements include the drawing-up of the Universal Declaration on the Human Genome and Human Rights, a text adopted by the General Conference of UNESCO at its thirtieth session. The second body, for its part, is being set up and its brief will include keeping a watchful eye to avoid any slip-ups with regard to the exploitation of scientific knowledge.

Moreover, with regard more specifically to the problems posed by information superhighways, UNESCO has set up a special task force on the "Ethics and Rights of Cyberspace", whose mission is to advise the Organisation on the "establishment at the international level of an ethical and legal framework for cyberspace and on the promotion of multi-linguism and cultural diversity in the new environment". I mention only these initiatives adopted by UNESCO to underline their relevance and to substantiate the earlier idea for the need to reform the UN. Indeed, all these laudable initiatives by UNESCO need to be supported by a genuine global power with a political and legal brief.

What Conclusions?

The absence of a genuine global authority can only strengthen the feeling of having to endure a form of Darwinism aggravated by globalisation. Globalisation itself does not make the poor richer; it does, however, widen even further the gap that separates the poor from the eternally wealthy. The ethics we are addressing here could more modestly be termed deontology, i.e. a minimum of rules pillared on universal principles of justice, equity, human solidarity beyond national borders, peace and protection of human dignity for all mankind. It is not a new practice; many of these rules already exist in the form of international conventions relating to various sectors of activity. The issue here, however, is to draw up new rules aimed at taming the risks of excesses by globalisation and at combating its barely concealed economic and informational Darwinism.

To achieve and satisfy the efficiency objective of this trend, national sovereignties will have to become less jealous of their prerogatives. When a torturer is questioned by the judicial authorities of a host country, under the clearly defined provisions of the 10 December 1984 Convention against Torture, how is it possible for the government of the country of which the torturer is a national to lodge a protest against such a procedure? Does the non-observance and non-ratification of such conventions justify certain states in opposing legal actions that are themselves fully justified? Is the spread of non-governmental organisations such as Amnesty International and Transparency International likely to raise the hope of finding a replacement for the failure of states? It is difficult to imagine so when one remembers that the state of Togo recently decided to lodge a complaint against the Secretary General of Amnesty International for propagation of incorrect information.

I still maintain that, more than ever before, the reform of the UN is a necessity if we do not want the 21st century to go on prolonging and sustaining the faults that existed at the close of the 20th century, particularly in matters of unbridled global liberalism. Ethical regulatory measures are needed, not only to ensure the observance of human rights but also to contribute towards reducing the impact of the law of the strongest on the economic affairs of the world.

Cultural Diversity at the National Level

BEATE WINKLER

What are the demands placed on us by globalization, particularly with regard to the peaceful co-existence of diverse cultures within one country? What standards should be upheld in such a context? How can we handle cultural differences more competently ourselves, and how can other people and institutions do likewise? What opportunities are afforded to us by cultural politics and the practice of culture which might support these efforts?

These questions need to be asked, for both the current situation and trends developing into the future show clearly that new approaches and a different consciousness are needed in cultural politics when the discussion focuses on the co-existence of a resident majority and those minorities who have arrived as immigrants, or on the co-existence of male and female migrants. We must engage with the fact that there will be increasing numbers of immigrant minorities, as a result of world-wide migrations from east to west and from south to north, and as a consequence of demographic development. Moreover, such migrant peoples will often be distinguished by a different sense of culture, and by different ethical values.

Alongside many positive developments in Europe and self-evident co-existence on a day-to-day basis, the relationship between resident and immigrant populations is also marked by uncertainty and withdrawal. The fear of a renewed spread of Islam has grown over recent years. On the part of the immigrant communities, there has been an equally steadily increasing fear of growing right-wing extremism and hostility towards foreigners. Engaging with these developments represents a challenge to our own sense of democracy. It is a form of global ethics operating at the national level: a decisive criterion in determining the value and the quality of a society's commitment to democracy lies in how that society treats ethnic, cultural and religious pluralism within its boundaries.

Today, as in the past, male and female migrants are still not entitled to participate in the life of society on an equal legal footing – despite the fact that this is an indispensable precondition for peaceful co-existence. Exclusion increases the sense of ethnic identity amongst minorities and encourages fundamentalist tendencies. It is particularly important to provide comprehensive measures aimed at integration and to communicate to minorities that they enjoy equal rights as part of a pluralistic society, given the background of modern transport and communication systems. Air travel and satellite television from the country of origin make it ever easier to remain culturally rooted in that country, practically to the exclusion of other cultures. The significance of this for cultural issues relating to co-existence has barely been investigated.

Addressing Opportunities, Contradictions and Policy Deficits

New ideas are needed to counteract a further polarisation between male and female migrants within a community, and to contribute to communication and understanding between people. Yet there are only a few approaches, at the practical or the political level, which have sought to strengthen the ability to handle cultural difference in a sensitive and responsible manner. Social institutions have only reluctantly taken on board the issues of intercultural dialogue. As in the past, the position on immigration continues to be largely a taboo subject, and too often there is an absence of clear policy statements on co-existence. Partly as a consequence of this, the ideas and strategies required in this area have barely been elaborated.

This policy deficit must also be judged against a background where questions of cultural co-existence are often experienced and judged in a contradictory way by the resident majority and the minorities coming from abroad. Where the immigrant culture is influenced neither by Western Europe nor North America, it is perceived by many people in Austrian society as threatening, especially if the culture draws on Islamic traditions. Many people show definite preferences for sameness and "homogeneity". They cannot cope with handling cultural difference sensitively and appropriately. As in the past, cultural "infiltration" is the most commonly expressed fear cited nowadays in surveys conducted throughout Europe. The fear of cultural infiltration is possibly also the most deep-seated of fears, because the "Other" is often seen as something threatening which cannot be incorporated and the sense of threat often first arises from an individual's own subjective feelings. The longing for a settled state of being, for minimal emotional disturbance and for harmony often leads an individual to deny the "otherness" of people, even over matters where an individual may himself experience inner conflicts due to uncertainty or ignorance. In doing so, the fact that the "Other" can also be exotic, fascinating and attractive is overlooked.

By contrast, some sections of society recognise that culture offers a special opportunity to influence co-existence in a positive way: culture in all its various forms – from art to popular culture – arises out of engagement with the "Other", providing the chance to experience diversity as something positive and helping to support efforts to handle contradictions and differences. This is an indispensable prerequisite for peaceful co-existence. Important personal skills can be strengthened through cultural work: tolerance, curiosity, or the ability to find unconventional solutions to problems. By engaging with the viewpoints of other people, one is in a position where one can put one's own attitudes into perspective and develop new approaches to finding solutions which bring together different views of the problem in hand. It is precisely these skills which are needed to solve the important challenges of the future. Given a society which is particularly susceptible to simple and radical ideologies, as a consequence of the thrust towards modernisation and the loss of traditional links, culture can create new links to people with a different cultural heritage through shared positive experiences. Cultural projects carried out jointly by male and female migrants not only offer the opportunity to counter prejudices on either side, but may also have an anti-discriminatory effect in the long-term because the viewpoints and experiences of male and female migrants are included, given equal status and provided with a forum for public expression. Moreover, we know from social and cultural history that the strongest sources of creative regeneration have often lain in precisely such engagement with, and working through, different cultural influences. The meeting of different cultures has almost always given rise to new developments.

There is a further aspect to this: culture supports the immigrant community as it finds its place in the new environment, providing a familiar space which is its own and which is necessary to enable that community to work through new and foreign experiences. As such, we are called upon to recognise prevailing cultural distinctions, not to devalue them. In cultural politics, the challenge will therefore be to formulate and implement a "policy of recognition". Such a policy means respecting these "Others" in terms of their identity and their prevailing and cultural distinctiveness, and accepting the "right to cultural difference". However, the right to cultural difference can lead to a clash of cultures if it involves a violation of human rights. Currently there is still no "global ethos" by which all peoples and all nations feel equally bound. The Rushdie situation clearly demonstrates this. Freedom of speech and tolerance are not universally accepted values. As such, one cannot speak of "unity in diversity" in the sense of taking the validity of human rights as a common element to which all peoples feel equally committed.

The growing discussion around the concept of a global ethos and transcultural ethics indicates that this is a desirable objective, one which is acquiring ever greater political importance and which should already be recognised today: after Auschwitz, our society has no alternative to the principle of "priority of human rights over the guiding values of other cultures". Our answer to the mass murder of European Jews cannot be to declare that human rights are optional. Culture clashes within our society should therefore be decided ultimately by reference to human rights. The question of the boundaries of tolerance, of determining what should and what should not be accepted, should be answered in accordance with human rights standards.

Providing Opportunities and Shaping Cultural Politics

Positive aspects arising from discussions of cultural politics must be given higher priority in public awareness. Public debate has focussed too one-sidedly on the aspect of "challenging hostility towards foreigners and opposing right-wing extremism", which has emphasised the negative aspect. All too often a "cloak of darkness" is thrown over cultural impulses, creativity, all that is stimulating, vital and controversial – the very sources from which new approaches are brought into being. The opportunity to use culture as a bridge and a means of understanding between the majority and the minorities, and to counteract any sense of threat, must be more clearly acknowledged. In many European countries, particularly over the past few years, a cultural scene has evolved which is shaped to a considerable extent by life in different cultures. This area of living culture is inadequately acknowledged by the established institutions. Participation on an equal footing remains the exception rather than the rule.

Setting issues of co-existence in a positive context is therefore just as necessary in the area of culture as in politics or the media – albeit without glossing over the real problems that exist, which happens all too often. Instead of addressing and dealing with fears and conflict situations arising from co-existence, these points are mostly discounted in public debates and labelled as examples of hostility towards foreigners – e.g. the fears of young people and their parents over reduced opportunities for education where there are high levels of immigrant schoolchildren in classes, or the fear of cultural infiltration in many areas of society. Failing to address such issues prevents the encouragement of known methods of taking positive action, such as developing the personal skills required to handle cultural difference more effectively.

Developing New Ways of Working Together

Positive and negative experiences must be brought together and presented in such a way that they can be of use in other places and in other areas of politics and life. The key problem to be resolved is the matter of communicating and translating to politics on a broader scale, and to society and the media, cultural experiences and the ideas and strategies applied in cultural politics. Many social groups remain too tight-knit and seek too little dialogue with people from other professional groups or other social backgrounds. Cultural transfer and essential networking are made more difficult as a result. There should be greater awareness that, in issues relating to co-existence between immigrant minorities and a resident majority, a highly complex set of questions are being addressed, which require complex answers. In coming to terms with globalisation, the decisive factor will be that people with different lifestyles and life experiences, different points of view and perceptions, generate new approaches together. In drawing up new ideas, strategies and projects, there are no ready answers; instead the process involves entering into a constant process of searching and asking questions: How can we strengthen the ability to handle cultural difference more sensitively and with greater responsibility? How can we succeed in altering our viewpoint and not considering our own perceptions and way of seeing things as the "centre of the world"? Can we cope with allowing others to be different, without blurring over those things which are divisive and alienating, and without making demands on others to conform or devaluing their otherness?

By engaging with other people, we experience a change in ourselves and we generally no longer make judgements based on our original sense of values. New things can develop. As part of this process, a fundamental precondition is that the resident majority and the immigrant minorities work together, and that male and female migrants co-operate to elaborate ideas, strategies and projects; it is similarly essential that there is a more intensive cultural exchange programme with the immigrants' countries of origin (e.g. exhibitions, grants programmes, joint theatre projects, translations). This process would be made easier if working groups were set up to accompany such exchanges, to take note of different interests in the relevant countries and to work out proposals for further initiatives. Given collaboration over the longer term, both problems and opportunities presented by globalisation and cultural exchange would be recognised more clearly and addressed in a positive manner. Not least, clashes of culture could be openly acknowledged and seen as a positive challenge for future development. Changed understanding of such clashes can lead to new approaches; this positive force deriving from conflict is appreciated too rarely. Conflicts which arise from different points of view can, admittedly, lead to painful situations. However, they can also be transformed into creative processes – into a productive dialogue between cultures. Politics and society are dependent on this dialogue if they are to do justice to their cultural diversity, in accordance with their democratic remit.

Summary

Globalisation requires us to increase intercultural dialogue and to exploit the major opportunities for co-existence offered in the cultural field in a responsible manner – without glossing over the associated problems. It is both incomprehensible and irresponsible if politicians still reinforce or even stir up fear of cultural infiltration, as often happens. The frequently asserted "homogeneity" of a national group neither exists today, nor has it ever existed in the past.

The challenge to cultural politics and the practice of culture is to work against such fear, both in its theoretical development and in its practical application. As part of this process, experiences are brought together and new forms of working together are explored. Instead of asserting a collision of cultures, the emphasis is on exploiting the major opportunities for cultural diversity and intercultural dialogue which globalisation presents. The prospects for the future in Europe lie in our cultural diversity and in intercultural dialogue.

Globality, Global Ethics and Indigenous Dignity

SAKEJ YOUNGBLOOD HENDERSON

All known life exists in a thin layer wrapped around the globe between the earth's molten core and the hostile cold environment of space. Although life extends from the oceans' deep trenches to the highest mountain peaks, what Indigenous peoples call the "living lodge" is no thicker than the shine on a billiard ball. The earth surface comprises only 30% of our water planet. About half of the land realm is hard to live upon. A third of the land realm is arid or semi-arid, eleven percent is the ice realm, where the land is permanently under ice, and ten percent is prairie tundra. Only 11% of the land is good for farming, and almost all of this is already in use. Most of the third of the land is seen as too poor, too thin, too wet to be of value to agriculture.

The continuing growth of the world's population fuels both the destruction of the environment and human destitution. The Brundtland Commission or the World Commission on Environment and Development found that rising poverty in poor countries and increasing pollution in rich ones are both unsustainable developments. This creates a tension on the existing lifestyles and standards that govern our lifestyles, especially international law, ethics and national laws. It demands a new moral and legal perspective of the land or of our linguistic and symbolic view of the land – the "langscape".

Very few, if any, states or regions exist in the world that do not have an enhanced plurality. Most nations are polyethnic and intercultural. Modern life is marked by a religious, intellectual, and cultural pluralism, yet in the Eurocentric discourse a deep ontology of fears exists about plurality, the different, the particular others. This is reflected in a commitment to singularity, the universal, the global, and the general. Eurocentric scholars have called this Christendom, Western civilization, Axial Period, Modernity, or now Global civilization. "Educated" Indigenous people refer to this as the "Eurocentric monologue".

Among colonized Indigenous peoples the Eurocentric monologue is labeled "Eurocentrism". For the last five centuries it has been an integral part of the academic professoriate, research, scholarship, and law. Eurocentrism postulates the superiority of Europeans over non-Europeans, based on two axioms: (1) most human communities are uninventive; and (2) only a few human communities (or places, or cultures) like Europe are inventive and remain permanent centers of cultural change or progress. From this base, the Eurocentric monologue asserts that the difference between the two sectors is that some intellectual or spiritual factor, something characteristic of the "European mind", the "European spirit", "Western Man", and so forth, leads to creativity, imagination, invention, innovation, rationality, and a sense of honor or ethics – in other words, "European values". The reason for non-Europe's non-progress is a lack of this intellectual or spiritual factor. This proposition asserts that non-European people are empty, or partly so, of "rationality", that is, of ideas and proper spiritual values. On a global scale, this gives us a

model of a world with a single center – roughly, Europe – and a surrounding periphery.
A strong critique of Eurocentrism is under way in all fields of social thought, revealing that the assumptions and beliefs which constructed the context are not universal and may be false.

Empires, states or nations which are constructed on a dominant ethnic identity have been abhorrent failures. The feigned neutrality of polyethnic states serves to reinforce the European male context at the expense of all others. An authentic state must mutually recognize and accommodate every culture in a respectful manner.

In the past decade, the reality of pluralism has created an expanded communication, a commitment to cross-cultural relativism and multicultural interactions. These interactions are Eurocentrism projecting itself on the other, by examining the difference by Eurocentric modes of analysis, and allowing the others who are trained in Eurocentric thought to project their voice to the other.

It is a way of becoming conscious of the cognitive and spiritual diversity of the living lodge, without confronting the process of cognitive and spiritual imperialism of the Eurocentric monologue. It is a way of transmitting information and exchanging ideas. Often "educated" Indigenous peoples refer to this as the "extended Eurocentric monologue" or "paradigm maintenance".

Eurocentric thinkers refer to the extended Eurocentric monologue as the "age of dialogue" or "age of global dialogue". "Educated" indigenous people honor the aspirational goal of transcultural dialogue, but do not think or feel that it has been achieved. The willingness to create such a dialogue is encouraging, it accepts and celebrates the need to grasp the unknown and uncertain, a way of creating a transformation in power and knowledge.

Occasionally the Eurocentric thinkers acknowledge the existence of prejudices against Indigenous or "local" thought or knowledge, but claim to be able to put them aside to understand Indigenous knowledge. However, despite good thoughts, from the standpoint of Indigenous knowledge such an approach limits understanding by refusing to acknowledge and explore inevitable internal prejudices rather than external object or thought. Because encounters with difference raises the validity of prejudgments, Indigenous peoples are best served by a personal examination of inherited and unreflectively held disabling prejudices, which allow one to transform obstacles and doubts to enable understanding of the unfamiliar other. Paradoxically, the concepts of pluralism, diversity, multiculturalism, difference, and the desire to understand exist as Eurocentric prejudices. They enable, cultural conventions of a Eurocentric consciousness that must be examined. They are not universal conventions, but rather embraced contraries.

The Eurocentric monologue never claimed to be a privileged regional norm, which would be an argument about cultural relativism. Instead, it claimed to be universal and general. It presents itself, and its diversity, as the ideal human type sanctioned by a singular God, nature or history. The European monologue has always held that

European civilization had two sources of inspiration that forbade Europeans to rest content with developing their own society and part of the world. The first inspiration was the Socratic search for knowledge. The other reason Europeans could not rest content with perfecting their own part of the world is the messianic prophecy of a millennium of monotheistic religions.

Around the globe, universality in the European monologue has created cultural and cognitive imperialism among Indigenous peoples, which established European knowledge, experience, culture, and language as the universal norm. The European scholarship, religion, or government were considered the embodiment of the universal, and had the privilege of not being considered as a member of any specific group. The anomalous ability of Eurocentric academics and lawyers to energize and legitimize the rhetoric of universalism in international law and colonial society was vast and remains powerful. It still prevents the human plurality from becoming empowered.

In the last two decades, I have actively worked toward linking power with plurality in the Canadian constitution and law, and in international law, especially the human rights fora. So I have experienced the ontology of fear and the need for singularity among powerholders, and understand the extended Eurocentric monologue is full of contradictions, tensions, and biases.

The powerful do not accept plurality as an operational principle. The most glaring example is Indigenous peoples and their inherent dignity, who have struggled to assert and prove they are human or entitled to human rights. The United Nations has not accepted that Indigenous peoples are entitled to human rights, and most national states have not treated Indigenous peoples as equals. Many reject their humanity and their dignity.

In addition, in the last two decades, I have attended many international and national conferences on the issue of building on plurality and towards a constructive pluralism. These conferences search for ways to affirm an inclusive democracy by affirming and honoring existing plurality and diversity. Yet, the processes of the conference often struggle against plurality, since there exists the idea that there are correct ways to think, feel and act. This tone relies on singularity or universal solutions, structures silence and inhabits the dialogue.

Pluralism in the ontology of fear arises from the question of whether "we" are ready to tolerate any system of values even when they are different from and in conflict with our own? Another fear is expressed more objectively: what are the transcultural criteria for evaluating plurality? The "we" asserts that tolerating intolerance undermines constructive tolerance, while the intolerance of intolerance defends constructive tolerance. Often, this fine distinction is called divisive or destructive plurality. In a global plurality, a troubling, fearful hermeneutic boundary exists between the constructive power of tolerance and the destructive outcome of preventing other people's view from being expressed in the public space of global ethics in a meaningful way. Yet, the "we" who raise the issue of tolerance is usually a self-appointed power or cultural elite, who assumes its superiority or bias based on singularity. This part of the global plurality has no inherent right or authority to silence other parts of the global plurality or to arbitrarily set the limits of tolerance as they did in the Eurocentric monologues.

From my experience, if we want to construct a shared humanity or a global ethic by a dialogue of power and plurality, the language of the dialogue must be fair and just. Its tone, the categories of each language, and the interpretative discourses of the inquiry must be fair and just.

This requires some renovation of prevailing Eurocentric assumptions and constructs of the cognitive reality and the world itself. We all understand the earth exists independently of the human senses, languages, ideologies, and our modes of analysis. The recognition of pluralities and multicultural people in structures or institutions of power requires a new fair dialogue about belonging and connecting energies.

In a fair dialogue of power and plurality, one can not build on the meta-narrative of colonization (the capitalist, socialist, or communist theories) or their gravity toward a singular (correct) solution or uniformity. Territorial sovereignty and the nation-state no longer define our cognitive world view; these artificial, classificatory concepts have lost their connective energies. They are used to create exclusive governments. Eurocentric governmental structures around the world developed from hierarchical principles of singularity that are aloof from citizens and do not form any sustainable connectedness beyond the election ceremony.

Because of the contagion of the Eurocentric monologue, the Eurocentric academic disciplines, their contrived languages or modes of analysis cannot solve most of the challenges of global plurality or even create a global consciousness. They may be relevant for a third of the human family, but are questionable as applied to the majority of the human family. An interdisciplinary or transdisciplinary approach may help to gain insights into plurality, but only new postcolonial interdisciplinary methods in the educational system will begin to solve the challenges of Indigenous knowledge and heritage.

A new "methodology" of experience and existence is required to synthesize and respect the global plurality. The Eurocentric constructs of "civilization", "culture", "identity", "civil society", "ethnic", "minorities", and "society" are not helpful in understanding global plurality. They are relics of the inherited normative vocabulary of Eurocentric thought and monologue and the empire of uniformity that sought to regulate the global "other". Each concept or trope a uni-dimensional slice of a multi-dimensional life world, and does not capture the inspiration or empowerment of human consciousness. These concepts are part of the problem of pluralism or globality.

Modern existence has an ephemeral quality, a fluid context, which renders the Eurocentric constructs unhelpful. No culture exists that is pure, exotic, separate, bounded and internally uniform. This Eurocentric version of culture seen as distinct billiard-balls has been transformed into an overlapping, interactive, internally negotiated, interculture or transculture. People live a continually contested, imagined, transformed, and negotiated existence, with an intertwining, extendable identity. The Eurocentric monologue appears inadequate for describing or contemplating realities or established guidelines of aggregation, even with the transcending metaphors of "trans" or "meta" or "supra-individual". Empathetic choice becomes the unavoidable reality of global plurality and the construction of cultural and self-determination of belonging and freedom. The culture or self is conceived as the interstices of intercultural dialogue.

There will always be those who are in-between these categories. They are contaminated constructs that emerge from a false viewpoint of Eurocentric singularity and a colonization theory (or the "European model of society"), and do not capture the interpenetration and convergence of individual desires and social values among all peoples of the living lodge. The extended Eurocentric monologue has not yet grasped the need to transform its thinking about multiculturalism to global plurality or the need for a sustainable connection with the ecology. In order to resolve ephemeral choices a new and fair dialogue is required.

In creating a fair dialogue about power and plurality, the participants have rejected the constructed dualism of "expert" and "non-expert", where the experts talk about "reality" and being. As Marshall McLuhan observed "the medium is the message". Despite good intentions, such constructed styles separate our search for connection, rather than building on this search. In their search for fair dialogues, participants need experiences in order to build such connections or convergences.

A fair dialogue must include respect for all languages and how they view relationships with the ecology and humans. A new multi-lingual consciousness must arise, that includes indigenous languages. We do not need a global Esperanto, but the protection and enhancement of more than fifteen thousand indigenous languages to help forge a new inter-cultural dialogue.

Recent studies have made it clear that Indigenous languages and worldviews are critically endangered. The linguist Ken Hale has estimated that half of the world's 6000 Indigenous languages are doomed because no children speak them. In the United States and Canada, the immigrants extinguished and replaced about 67% of Aboriginal consciousness with Eurocentric consciousness. Recent studies in Canada show that all fifty-three Aboriginal languages are critically endangered. Only three Aboriginal languages in Canada have a chance of surviving into the next century.

Consciousness and language have created global and local plurality, but this crucial power has not been examined sufficiently. All too often Indigenous consciousness and languages have been suppressed and abused to nourish singularity. The exclusive privileging of some languages has been a means of nourishing singularity and xenophobia. The essence of inclusive dialogues is a constructive achievement of learning with different languages and their structure. This is a respectful and reflective way to engage, care, and connect with cognitive plurality and empathetic learning that creates multi-layered transcultural meanings. After constructing a fair and equitable dialogue, a manifesto of global ethics can be created. Space must be created for

Indigenous languages. From an Indigenous peoples' experience and perspective the manifesto must unfold several principles.

The first principle of global ethics must be that within the world of unseen power, all life, in all its forms, is our relatives. Humans must face their ontology of fear or forever run or hide from it.

A second principle must acknowledge the duty to preserve and enhance all endangered languages of the world. A search of global ethics cannot be exclusive, and inclusive dialogue requires saving all endangered languages, understanding their structure and wisdom. Languages are usually the voice of the belonging, loving, sharing and caring, what we call the "sounds of the heart" that was given for good deeds. People need to learn how to talk in different languages, then learn how to teach each other. Teaching must come from sharing what is within, instead of without; that is an Indigenous essence of an age of dialogue.

A third principle is that people must not judge others until they have learned their language, and lived with them for several seasons. The golden rule is an imaginative construct, but humans need the experience of the others to understand how to relate to humans.

A fourth principle is that people must walk their talk, not create "ought to be" ideologies or utopian empires. Deeds are more important than words. An age of dialogue must be built doing and being such "halo" or fuzzy words as trust, good faith, caring, and a desire to share and learn.

A fifth principle is that all religions, ideologies, and beliefs are necessary to understand the Life-giver's plurality, and not to create a false singularity or necessity. The Life-giver has made us what we are; it is not her will that we should be changed or made uniform. It makes no difference as to the name of the Life-giver, since creating life is an endless process.

Global Ethics in Practice

ANDREAS UNTERBERGER

Certain rules of human, political and economic coexistence are so important as to make their application beyond individual cultures imperative in our unavoidably globalised world. These rules are closely associated with individual ethical norms, be they grounded in philosophy, religion or legal positivism. Global ethics must, for one, be based on individual ethics and be compatible with them; for another, their aim must be dignity for every human being on Earth. As a social, a collective set of rules, however, their contents differ from those of individual ethical norms.

Their most essential codification thus far is to be found in the classic catalogues of human rights, in the European Convention on Human Rights and in the UN Covenant on Civil and Political Rights. Much of what has been added to these catalogues since (human rights in the "second, third or fourth generation") may be desirable, such as the worldwide right to health, but is not implementable as a norm the way freedom of speech is. These constantly expanding catalogues have therefore only led to a dilution of these most fundamental of postulates. The latter represent not European, not American, not Asian but global fundamental principles. It is acceptable that Asians might find specific forms of western democracy alien to their culture. It is untenable, however, when many an Asian government asserts that repudiation of torture or the right to express one's own opinion and practice one's own religion is contrary to "Asian values." (This platitude about Asian values is shared only by the governments, not by independent intellectuals.)

It is true, however, that these fundamental rules have thus far been brought to fruition only in Europe. This achievement marks an historical quantum leap forward for the old continent. It was in Europe that norms on human rights were rendered judicially and above all supranationally enforceable for the first time in history. Here, for the first time ever, individuals are no longer helpless objects of state power. Probably the most dangerous flaw in the current world order is the absolutism claim of the currently (in this case truly globally) prevailing concept of state encapsulated in the word "sovereignty", a principle so highly valued in international law. The progress of Western Europe is marked by the fact that for the first time ever citizens can now appeal to a non-governmental authority that stands above the state. From these fundamental considerations, one can draw several postulates as touchstones for discussion in the search for a catalogue of global ethics.

1. As in Europe, the observance of fundamental human rights must be monitored and adjudicated world-wide (also in North America!) by courts of appeal which are independent of the states and whose rulings must be binding on the states.

2. In our efforts to control financial flows, protect the environment, fight against regional or world-wide monopolies, achieve minimum social rights, we need, first, a global legislature and, second, a global judiciary. This legislature must be subject to very narrow limits so that our need to render several fundamental rules enforceable world-wide

does not give way to excess regulation that would rob Third World states of their comparative advantages in trade; so that over-regulation itself does not diminish and dilute the most important of the minimum standards.

3. Equally important is the expansion of ethical, religious or linguistic rights for groups. The kind of minority protection required in this regard is (incompletely) codified in Europe yet not actionable before courts of law. Meeting this demand would do more than merely serve the ethical postulate that minorities be given complete equality to practice their language, culture and religion on all levels, i.e. not just in folk dancing groups. Protecting minorities and recognising autonomy claims would also be the most important steps we could take for safeguarding world peace. After all, unresolved ethnic conflicts are the main cause of contemporary wars.

4. On a par with this demand is the one calling for the establishment of norms and channels to enforce the right of self-determination. This too is a peace policy and at the same time democracy in its most perfect form: It is a violation of human dignity when citizens can elect the persons and parties who govern a state but are not allowed to decide to which state their religion belongs. As an initial step, a catalogue must be drawn up defining from what size, with what quorum and in what gravity (for example by means of a referendum to be repeated at a minimum set interval) a group may declare their secession. As a second step, an international board of arbitration must be set up to resolve disputes.

5. A central demand of global ethics is that states cease acting as adjudicative organs and act instead as executive organs to enforce the legal rulings of a world system. In this

sense, the veto right in the UN Security Council may reflect the prevailing power structure but it certainly does not meet ethical requirements. Thus: democratisation and codification of the embryonic attempt of the UN into a world system, which has turned out to be a seriously handicapped monstrosity. As a journalist, I would like to add several media policy demands to these briefly outlined global political demands. A large number of media in many places have been progressively trivialised and corrupted to a frightening degree. Television executives, publishers and journalists are called upon as occupational groups to fulfil several very serious ethical imperatives. Yet history shows that giving government great power to intervene in the media has even more devastating consequences. The central demand for global media ethics is therefore one which has been a cornerstone of human rights since the very outset, namely, freedom of expression and freedom of the media.

6. Safeguarding the freedom and diversity of the media requires additional state or EU action beyond current media law in an area heretofore neglected in many countries, namely, better regulations for preventing media concentration and for breaking up cartels.

7. All the norms needed to regulate media operations should be administered not by state authorities but by independent media institutions. This is the only way to guarantee the independence of the media.

8. The excessive data protection practised in many countries has proven to be an obstacle in fighting corruption, achieving transparency and having law enforcers adopt a more service oriented attitude. It should be replaced by the Swedish model under which all government files are completely open to the public.

The following principles apply to all of the postulates named:

9. Since they are not likely to be implemented in the near term world-wide, it should be recommended that states striving to put global ethics into place enter first into binding conventions themselves. With these states as role models, functioning structures would soon attract non members.

10. A part of development assistance should be specially earmarked for states that submit to the minimum requirements set down for global ethics and good governance. This includes the application of anti-corruption laws and the development of functioning markets.

Global ethics will remain an illusion heard only in Sunday speeches by politicians so long as they are not implemented in the concrete steps outlined above. All concepts that limit themselves to the legal re-education of people while disregarding the legal or organisational framework of the state sovereignty era are bound to fall short of the mark.

Informed to Death or Entertained to Death?

Peter Pelinka

Relentless in his warnings about the media apocalypse, the American media analyst Neil Postman makes regular mention in his books of "infotainment", the modern mix of information and entertainment. Our day-to-day lives together as human beings, he says, have been rendered more brutal as our communications have become more trivial, leading to an even more serious result, the drying up of ethical values. To him, it is irrelevant whether we sit before a TV or computer screen amusing ourselves or entertaining ourselves to death. Regardless of whether one shares Postman's cultural pessimism or not, the ethical question as to whether journalistic reporting of violence is necessary for curtailing it appears to be more topical than ever, as does the debate whether "staged" or artistic treatment of violence per se does not perforce foster it. What relationship is established here between the media and violence? What (media) policy conclusions can be drawn in this regard from the ethical principle that says we should live together as freely of violence as possible? Cloaked in more positive terms: What part could the media play in enforcing global ethical principles, assuming they should do more than merely legitimise strategic, and heretofore also highly unethical, interests?

1. Violence and the media:
Children and adolescents shooting at others without blinking an eye? Not children soldiers in so-called Third World countries, but camouflage-clad US high school kids running amok, cold-bloodedly selecting victims among their fellow students? The media is often singled out for blame when an event like this occurs. However, such acts are attributable first and foremost to real weapons, especially in the US, which has nearly as many weapons in circulation as it has inhabitants. Only by eliminating easily accessible "private" weapons will people be kept from using them to kill others. An example from Austria: A 15 year-old from Lower Austria who shot his teacher in 1998 had only to take his father's gun out of a cardboard box. Following a shooting spree that ended in a blood bath last year, the English government drew some clear-cut conclusions and banned all handguns. But the declining inhibitions about violence on the part of many young people is partially also attributed to certain media. In computer and video games, for example, the object is still usually to eliminate as many opponents as possible. At some point, the line between reality and game can begin to blur. The same conclusions have been drawn by international researchers on youth: As a whole, young people in western societies are less violent today than in the past, but among a small group of them violence has increased. Their threshold for violence is lower. Udo Jesionek, chief presiding judge of the Austrian Juvenile Court, believes the daily depiction of violence in the media, especially on TV, "cannot leave people totally unaffected."

Nonetheless, the availability of a weapon is a much more important determinant of whether a dispute ends in death.

How do the media cover violent scenes in general? All television sets in the US with a screen larger than 33 cm have what is called a V-chip built in as a standard component. Depending on how "sensitively" the parents set the chip, it can block shows and render them inaccessible for children. The big "but" is that a producer or TV station must code the programs and define their suitability for a given age group. Jay Hamilton, a professor at Duke University in North Carolina, issues a warning in this regard: Corporate groups do not want to place TV ads before programs labelled as violent. For this reason, many stations merely give their series and films the lapidary label of "suitable for 16 and above."

The Austrian media psychologist Peter Vitouch believes "the output of violent films could tend to increase because of the V-chips." Although it has been proven that "violence in the media is not beneficial", it cannot be made directly and completely responsible for actual violent acts. Children learning to cope with fear and feelings of danger is a major part of growing up. However, it is important that children have a relationship with their parents that can help them to reduce the fear the media make them feel. Neil Postman has been preaching a stricter and more one-dimensional message for two decades: Virtual worlds and trivialised real brutalities compete with each other – especially in the minds of children and adolescents. Individuals who are growing up and going through puberty cannot handle this situation. This is particularly true when there is a highly complex relationship between producer and consumer. A 1997 UNESCO study involving interviews with 5000 twelve year-old pupils from 23 countries found that violent action heroes are among the most popular idols of young people. Eighty-eight percent of them were familiar with Arnold Schwarzenegger in his role as the "Terminator". More than one-third of those asked wanted "to be like him" according to this study on media violence; the figure rose to one-half in crisis regions. Joe Groebel, the author of the study, concluded that depictions of violence in the media contribute to an aggressive culture. Television is the number one leisure activity for children. In Europe, 99 percent of them have access to a TV set; in Africa, 83 percent. According to this study, teenagers world-wide watch TV on average three hours a day. Groebel found that young people are limited in their ability to distinguish between medium and reality. Forty-six percent of children living in violent environments (areas where civil war is raging) assumed that the two overlap.

Europe, too, is trying to take legal action in this area. The EU has called on its member states to develop media protection guidelines for young people. Gerhard Weis, director of the ORF (Austrian Broadcasting Company) always refers in this context to the careful way the ORF handles scenes of violence. The ORF has in fact imposed its own guidelines which have been further reinforced by an ORF coding system for all films. Weis rejects a state-run "public censorship commission" as a token action, demanding instead that politicians and the media take concrete steps to reduce violence in society.

The effects violence in modern media has on people are undisputed.

– They satisfy collective and individual needs for violence suppressed by civilisation processes and help to counter daily feelings of helplessness.

– In some consumers, they reinforce the tendency to equate media staged violence with actual experiences of violence.

– They reinforce the tendency to accept and tolerate violence actually occurring in society, particularly by causing people to lose their sense of empathy.

Of course it is also agreed that there are no hard and fast formulae for countering these trends, except perhaps careful and thorough reflection. As surely as legal regulations are essential in certain areas, isolated calls for censure are bound to remain ineffective. As psychiatrist Stephan Rudas says: "We live in an age of overdose." He is referring primarily to an overdose of violence in everyday life, including that doled out in the media. But do the media trigger or reinforce violence, are they dangerous in and of themselves or could they be a useful relief valve? Even university professor Bernhard Rathmayer, who believes the media are responsible for the growing propensity to violence, notes in his book *Von der Faust ins Auge* (From Fist to Eye): "Empirical research on the effects of the media indicates only that neither possibility can be excluded: violent media may either decrease or increase violence in those who partake of it." The research findings do show that violence in the media can have negative effects on certain high risk groups, such as children without a stable home life or with serious psychological problems. However, according to Rathmayer, "It is not a foregone conclusion that the consumption of violence in the media alone triggers aggressive action or, conversely, that the aggression in society causes people to want to consume violence in the media". And it is by no means certain what part "politics" plays in reinforcing or curbing the development of violence in society or whether they can even play a part.

The issue is further complicated by the unique problems associated with documenting real violence. The news is not specially coded. The V-chip will not interpret bloody footage of a real war in a news show as a danger to young children. TV news in general is a sensitive area when it comes to violence. To what extent is it necessary to show actual violence in a report? What is sensationalism and what is the unavoidable price to pay for informing the public about bad events? Many felt that the ZDF, a major German station, failed to walk this fine line a year ago. In its 7 p.m. news show *Heute*, a clip was shown of soldiers in the Congo throwing a man from a bridge and then shooting him. Johannes Fischer, the man in charge of ZiB2 and ZiB3, the 7.30 and 10.00 o'clock ORF evening news programs in Austria, responded to the incident as follows: "I would certainly not allow a murder occurring before the camera to be broadcast." The line is very hard to draw in certain instances. "You have to make the decision on a case by case basis after viewing the pictures. When the UN found the mass graves, we broadcast pictures of them." But this cannot be done merely for the sake of showing the pictures. This is a problem that goes beyond the ethics of individual journalists. More than ever before, from the Gulf to Kosovo, from Somalia to Rwanda, political decisions are made on the basis of public sentiment, even at the international level. And more than ever before, this sentiment is shaped by the way the media reports the events, giving the media a significant political role.

2. The difficulty of understanding a globalised world:
Our information situation today is very akin to what Sigmund Freud described as "oceanic" in *Civilisation and Its Discontents* in reference to the awareness of modern mankind, e.g. fluctuating, floating, yet also global. In this age of satellite TV, mobile phones and the Internet, we have more possibilities than ever before to assemble as large a mosaic of information as we wish. At the same time the world has been rendered even less understandable by these new technologies; a reality is created that less and less resembles our everyday lives. We receive an increasing amount of information yet are less capable of assimilating it all. We can find out at any time how many people died in a hurricane that passed through the Philippines just hours before; we see babies in Africa starving before our very eyes; we see how American bombs drift seemingly peacefully towards Iraqi targets and somewhat less peacefully towards Yugoslavian ones, like a video game. We learn that the new technologies have drastically reduced the information monopoly while increasing our risk of being manipulated. The competition among the media appears to reduce this risk somewhat yet we know that the flow of information is ever more standardised and dependent upon strategic and economic interests. The whole world is informed about certain crises for a certain length of time while other crises occurring around the world are simply faded out. Even battles and dying appear to submit to the laws of the media world, the necessary mix of bad news and good news, the cyclical popularity of topics. Yet battles and dying continue even after the spotlight shifts away from them.

3. The waning significance of traditional politics:
The overall significance of traditional politics is waning everywhere. In modern societies, politics can no longer claim to be the sole and central instrument of societal control. Today the political system is one functional system alongside many others, alongside the economy, the media, culture, religion. It is becoming steadily less important. Today the political system is no longer the supreme system in control of all other subsystems, it has become itself a subsystem in an ever more complex, fragmented, differentiated and more difficult to control society. The waning significance of traditionally conducted politics becomes clear when it is compared to the media, which have long since gone beyond their initial function of mere reporting to become an active subsystem which also shapes politics. The media set agendas, determine what topics and discussions occur, control or at least promote political and societal trends by going to extremes in personalising them and spearheading campaigns for or against them.

– The economy, whose ups and downs from boom to recession, whose international interdependence and lobbies are steadily narrowing the leeway for action in shaping politics, particularly on the national level.

– Culture, especially the electronic mass culture, global images of "stars" and life styles created and reinforced in keeping with the motto "idols, not ideals."

It is only in comparison with other institutions "that instil meaning", such as the traditional churches, that politics has not lost in relative significance. These institutions are exhibiting similar deficits. The crisis of ideologies is apparent everywhere.

4. The Americanisation of politics:
In parallel with these other trends, politics is becoming Americanised. Parties are losing their traditional function as foundations of the political system. They are being challenged in their social function by other institutions in the Information and Entertainment Society, in their function of selecting political elites by other (group, media) mechanisms, in their function as ideological bonding instruments by an ever more pluralistic and fragmented society. When this development has run its course, what is left is a political system like the American one, whose "parties" often constitute nothing more than accidental sums of the "vested rights" of individual "representatives of the people". The natural consequence is a personalisation of politics. Topics and parties are then apparently only "sellable" with individual celebrities; politicians become "show stars" like any other in the entertainment business. "Media parties" are created around a strong central figure with virtually no organisational structure involved. At the same time, the "career phases" of politicians are shortened. Stars rise to the top faster than ever before only to plunge into obscurity all the sooner. Naturally, the better a "cast", the greater the success. "Cast" is meant here in two senses: A person/party "standing" for one or more topics, one or more social or cultural issues, one or more values and able to become the central player in this discussion and also able to meet all the criteria of a good actor in performing the role, able to come across as authentically as possible, also in private roles. When the person and role are right, when the topic and the values are on the mark, this successful vehicle can afford to remain on the political stage for an extended run, even in the face of critical media reviews and despite inevitable signs

of wear around the edges. Moreover, it will be credited as being steadfast and reliable for doing so. Politicians and politics become merchandise that has to be sold as effectively as possible. The status of the media, the advertising and PR industry is enhanced to the same extent as staging and styling are required to be "just right." At its most grotesque, the system renders almost irrelevant what a politician says; he can even afford to switch "values" on central issues along with the crowds of potential voters he is addressing, as long as he retains his general gestures and posture. Case in point: Haider's role as the rebellious crocodile in Austrian domestic politics.

5. Internationally, societies of the western developed variety are in the process of turning from democracies into mediocracies. Indications thereof are the public's obvious lack of enthusiasm for parties and politics, the rise of populism, the need for issues to be "marketable", the decrease in participation. The media now serve as the crucial plane between the actors and the audience of politics. In fact, they are increasingly amassing their own direct political influence. In keeping with the "structural change of the public" (described by Jürgen Habermas back in 1962), "political marketing" is replacing conscious politicising of the people, the attempt to win over and mobilise the masses for a certain idea.

6. Television has taken the lead among all media in this development since the beginning of the 1990's. It has changed social customs, the political systems and the rest of the (print) media in decisive ways, especially with regard to the distinction between "information" and "entertain-

ment." Catchwords here are "reality TV", "the personalisation of politics", "the sensationalisation of society." In the mid-1990's, television was finally supplanted in its role as the leading medium by the computer, or to be more precise, by the multimedia combination of television, telephone, computer, Internet, scanners, and CD-ROM. This merging of computers, telecommunications and television is now also referred to as the "Negroponte implosion" after Nicholas Negroponte, the director of the media laboratory at the Massachusetts Institute of Technology. A milestone along the highway to "cyberspace", to "artificial intelligence", to the "Virtual Society", to the "global village", as the litany of new concepts associated with this modern media debate read.

7. At the same time, the media sector along with all other aspects of society are being relentlessly capitalised through and through. This means the economic forces of the market are displacing the political forces of laws. Politicians are being driven by the media, are acquiescing to them, and everything is inundated with advertising.

The media and communications industry is the fastest growing of all economic sectors. The Information Society is beginning to replace the Industrial Society. More and more people are working in the tertiary sector (in the US, already one-third of the workforce), fewer and fewer in the secondary (industrial) sector and the fewest of all in the primary sector (agriculture). In Europe alone, 60 million jobs will be directly associated with telecom in the year 2000. Consequently, the process of concentration is the greatest in this sector; only a handful of huge corporations or publishing houses can survive. One way they are doing so is by increasingly interlinking media capital in the printing and electronics sector (TV, radio). The major providers of capital in the Information Society operate on a global level and are concentrated in both senses of the word. Murdoch, Bettelsmann, Kirch, Disney, Turner all invest gigantic sums in acquisitions, data highways, film rights, use of satellites, publishing houses. This in turn leads to a concentration of subject matter. Fewer and fewer topics are being "aired" world-wide with all the more vigour; it is becoming increasingly difficult to place "anti-cyclical" subjects such as development policy in the media.

8. Global markets require new forms of consumerism. As a media consumer, instead of receiving individual products, a person pays for the use of a virtual public locality: Pay TV is replacing video; encyclopaedias or databases on CD-ROM are supplanting shelves of books or phone directories; films on demand are fast winning out over set TV programming schedules. These new offerings do not signal the death of television, only its expansion, made possible by digitisation. Viewers are no longer limited to 20 stations, they can now receive 500 or 600 different ones. This is the reason so much hope is being placed in TV decoders as a product innovation while the computer industry must now reduce itself to a healthier size. The societal consequences are both positive and negative. The use of new media on the labour market is creating a more flexible workforce, offering women in particular more opportunities for part-time jobs and transforming traditional office hierarchies into relatively independent sets of mobile phone and laptop workers. Moreover,

dic-tatorial systems are rendered impossible, outmoded communications structures are at last cast aside, creating at least a chance for world-wide information. On the other hand, workers who are not so well informed, not so flexible, and not so young have fewer opportunities than ever; the gap in society between the informed and the uninformed is widening. The complete privatisation of the entertainment industry has led to its complete commercialisation: A dramatic concentration of media, a decline in quality in some quarters, a diminishing respect for privacy and the rights to privacy. There is also a trend towards expropriating the public. Leo Kirch just put down DM 3.4 billion for the television rights to the soccer world championships in 2002 and 2006; Rupert Murdoch handed over DM 2 billion for the rights to broadcast the champions league for his German station tm3 starting in the coming season. The logic behind these moves is that only high viewer ratings guarantee high ad revenues. Sports events, as social mass phenomena, guarantee high ratings and enable access that requires individual payments (pay TV). The intention of this seizure of sports is to make new stations popular, for who will prevent tycoons from purchasing the rights to a crime, to war coverage or to a sermon? "If the political community does not act, fees will be charged first for sports and then for other current events," warns the German communications and political expert Peter Glotz. The British House of Lords decided, for example, that sports events of national significance must be made accessible to the public at large.

9. Conclusions:
There is an impending threat of a telecracy based on internationalisation, privatisation and commercialisation. This form of remote domination, comparable to bureaucracy, is brought about by the intelligent linkage of telematics, goods production, trade and modern services. It cannot be countered by anti-media fundamentalism but only by means of an intelligent communications policy dedicated to rendering modernisation civilised, a policy completely free of great power political fantasies (which would be senseless anyway given the world-wide technical and economic developments) and cynical wait-and-see attitudes (Norbert Bolz: "We should risk the idea that the evening gathering around the magically flickering tube is akin to a post-modern version of the primordial hordes around their campfires"). Media policy must be expanded to create a communications policy. Below are several aspects necessary for this change, though the list is by no means exhaustive:

– Controlled development of information super highways (attempts at which are being practised by the US government under Al Gore's leadership);

– More intensive use of computers and media analysis in schools;

– Promotion of interactive forms of communication like the Internet by lowering phone rates (problems: data and other protection measures);

– Regulations for advertising and against concentration (no general ban on cross ownership but complete disclosure of ownership structures);

– Safeguarding the role of the public sector as indispensable in conveying national culture in an international concert and in acting as a counterweight to the private commercial sector.

The World as a Global Living Room

ALEXANDER WRABETZ

The world has become a village – a global village. This has been known, at the latest, since the Gulf War of 1991, when around the world it was possible to view and experience direct broadcasts of Iraqi cities being bombed as part of operation "Desert Storm". This was war viewed from the sofa – the world as a global living room.

The triumphant march of the Internet has enormously strengthened this tendency towards the global village. Whilst in Austria a home equipped with cable or satellite TV can receive an average of 33 channels, and in some households up to 75 channels, Internet users are literally presented with the whole world at their fingertips. For example, if users want to find out about the current situation in Kosovo and about the background to the conflict, the Internet offers them the home page of the Serbian Information Ministry alongside the home page of the KLA (the liberation army of the Kosovan Albanians), and the home page run by the charity organisation "Nachbar in Not" (*Neighbour in Need*). The whole world is only a mouse-click away.

The Internet offers completely new possibilities to broadcasting companies like Austria's ORF (Österreichischer Rundfunk). Until recently, the ORF broadcast its programmes exclusively on analogue terrestrial channels, thereby limiting the broadcasting area – the Österreichischer Rundfunk was largely broadcasting to Austria.

In 1994, the ORF co-founded the European cultural broadcasting channel 3sat with the German broadcaster ZDF (Zweites Deutsches Fernsehen) and the Swiss broadcaster SRG (Schweizerische Radio- und Fernsehgesellschaft). In 1998, the ORF gradually began broadcasting its programmes via digital satellites. With these satellite activities, the ORF is also increasingly coming to mean broadcasting from Austria. Broadcasting to and from Austria also takes place on the World Wide Web, with the highly successful Internet channel ORF ON. Two years after it was set up, ORF ON is one of the most regularly visited web addresses in Austria, and a clear market leader amongst Austrian content providers. In March 1999, ORF ON returned record figures of nearly 9 million page views (the precise figure was 8,991,646) and 3.66 million visits. Without being primarily designed for that purpose, ORF ON is also highly successful in the international market: the Austrian Internet channel ranks amongst the "top ten" content providers in the entire German-speaking Internet market.

Although this service is an offshoot of the ORF's core business, Internet services are increasingly developing into a medium in their own right. Against all forecasts, however, Internet services are yet to be a means of making money. Nevertheless, the motto being applied is "it's not the winning, it's the taking part". It is of crucial importance for the future of the ORF that it follows and sets future trends. As the largest national media company, the ORF must maintain a presence in the medium of the future, the Internet.

The success of the ORF ON shows that ORF can legitimately claim to be active in the area of new media. That success also shows, however, that the Internet audience appreciates quality, and that quality will win out in the end.

Global Media – Global Ethics?

The Internet is a completely democratic medium and knows no national boundaries: anyone with a PC has access to the world. Similarly, anyone who wishes to do so can set up their own website. To communicate around the world, you no longer need a lot of money, simply the necessary know-how. This is one of the most significant differences with traditional media – printing, radio and television – which specifically require capital to get started.

The easy availability of and straightforward access to the Internet are what make this medium so fascinating. The Internet respects no national boundaries. Bans and attempts at censorship prove ineffective when it comes to the Internet. The Internet is an absolutely democratic medium. For example, when the independent Belgrade radio broadcaster B 92 was banned from broadcasting by the Serbian government, the programme makers switched to using the Internet and were able to continue their independent reporting, unimpaired by Slobodan Milosevic and his Serbian hardliners. However, the fact that this medium is so completely resistant to censorship can also lead to misuse. The main areas where this occurs are child pornography, neo-Nazi activities, and instructions on bomb-making.

There is currently much debate about misuse of the freedoms afforded by the Internet, and about attempts to combat such misuse.

Where the misuse involves criminal activities conducted over the Internet, such as participating in child pornography rings, the matter is clear. The appropriate national authorities have a duty to intervene and to put an end to such abuses.

Over and above that, can and should the Internet, which is spread world-wide, be subject to supranational rules and regulations?

In my opinion, this is neither desirable nor even possible in practice. Although the world is increasingly becoming a global village, that village has no unified ethical standards. The global village is multiethnic and multicultural. The most diverse traditions, philosophies, religions and patterns of behaviour all flow together here. Apart from certain basic principles, such as those incorporated in the United Nations' Charter on Human Rights, there is no system of ethics binding upon the whole world. Things which are permissible in a European country will perhaps be frowned upon in an Arab country, and the reverse is similarly true. Cultural traditions are too diverse to be simply cut to the same length using the same global measurement. The danger is too great that a ban on debate will be issued in the name of global ethics, and that the dynamics of the new media will be restricted.

Who would police the laws to be applied world-wide for the Internet? In an era of world-wide communication, wanting to set up a kind of global Internet-police or Internet-censorship would give a fundamentally wrong message. Anyone doubting this should consider that the positive aspects of the global network outweigh the disadvantages represented by excesses which may be wholly unattractive, but which are ultimately marginal to the network as a whole.

In the Internet, as with other media, the key element is responsibility. However, responsibility cannot be achieved through legislation, but can only be arrived at through a permanent learning process.

In this context, I would refer to the debate about violence in the media, and particularly on television. At an inquiry conducted by the ORF and the Austrian Ministry for the Family in March 1999 entitled "Violence in the Media", speakers and those contributing to discussions unanimously agreed that broadcasting companies, parents and teachers had a shared responsibility to work towards a society which was as free of violence as possible. According to the opportunities afforded to them, all should seek to educate children and young people to deal responsibly with the topic of violence and violence in the media.

This shared responsibility, and the responsibilities divided up according to areas of competence between parents and school in addressing the topic of violence on television, could also serve as a model for the Internet. Just as a child should not be left sitting on his or her own in front of the television, so a child should not be left alone with the PC. Schools should give greater attention to the new Internet medium as part of their focus on media education.

Last but not least, there is a responsibility which devolves upon the content providers. As an example, let us consider the Internet activities of the ORF. As a public media corporation with a legally defined remit, the ORF also functions as an independent and objective content provider in its Internet presence. Via the Internet, public service broadcasting can demonstrate its standards to a world-wide audience. Other public service broadcasting corporations in Europe, and notably the BBC, offer content under such a remit, which carries with it a particular sense of responsibility.

The Role of Public Service Broadcasters as Internet Content Providers

The Internet is a new medium and, as such, is a complementary rather than a substitute medium. In Austria alone, around two million people are able to take part in this world-wide data exchange – yet despite this, the numbers of those listening to radio or watching TV are not falling. The Internet represents an ideal and also an essential extension to radio and TV, particularly for public service broadcasting corporations, which are not geared to maximising profits but to content and matters of public interest instead. Without committing large amounts of funds or staff, key tasks forming part of the legal duties of the public service broadcaster in the fields of politics, economics, culture, education and science, religion and sport, can also be delivered on the World Wide Web.

Public service broadcasting companies on the Internet offer reliable information and can be depended upon by the user, who is often faced with a confusing plethora of sources in this medium.

However, there are attempts being made by commercial media to obstruct the activities of public service broadcasters in the Internet through legal regulations. In their view the Internet, being a new medium, should be exclusively available for use by private commercial interests. This overlooks the fact that competition in the Internet does not take place between commercial and public service broadcasting companies, but is influenced to a vast extent by the emergence of, for example, technology and communications companies.

Public service broadcasting companies are a guarantee of

diversity of opinions, of objectivity and of independence in the face of the advances being made by "non-media companies" as far as content is concerned.

As examples of such advances, consider the attempts made by Microsoft, now seeking to transform itself from being the most powerful software company into being an approved content provider as well, or the measures taken by various telephone companies who are seeking to play a dominant role in the Internet market.

Neither telephone companies nor software companies have a tradition of journalistic ethics and professionalism behind them, merely the desire to extend their scope for generating added value by deploying large capital sums in a short time-frame. As a complement to these new giants in the field of the Internet, an independent presence of public service broadcasting providers is both sensible and necessary. These Internet presences will also take the form of alliances between public service and private media companies.

In summary, I would like to stress again the following points: there can be no global ethics and no global authorities enforcing ethics for the Internet. Ethics are always culturally and historically determined, and for that reason they always assume different forms.

The positive effects of the development of the new media outweigh the dangers of excesses. Where there is doubt, the benefit of the decision should go to the freedom of the new media.

It is also an absolute necessity to have public service broadcasters as content providers on the World Wide Web. The key word here is content. For public service broadcasters, the bottom line is the content and the message; for commercial content providers, the bottom line is the financial return on outlay.

A dual system of media presence, as a parallel structure of public service and private media providers, will prove to be sensible for the Internet, as for other media.

How Global Are Global Values?

KRZYSZTOF ZANUSSI

George Soros noted that people living in democracies do not necessarily view democracy as a universal concept in which they believe. Although it is true that these concepts also have to do with human rights and so forth, most democracies in Europe are global democracies. Our democracy is good enough.

I was recently in Minsk, the capital of Belarus, and met a diplomat from a European country whose name I won't mention for fear of denunciation. He told me there was a vast difference between Russia and Belarus. Russia was much, much worse off. I asked why and he said: Here there is a little bit of democracy. To organise a large concert, I have to bribe people. In Belarus that is very easy; there is just a single person to bribe while in Russia I have to bribe many different people. Now, this was a good citizen of the West who said his own democracy was good; he did not want to have to pay bribes in his society but elsewhere it was ok.

When we point out that many values are good for us yet do nothing to change the values of others, to pass on our own values, we are engaging in ethical relativism. My tendency would be to say that fundamental values throughout the world are the same. One could cite religion as a counterexample, cite the example of the Inquisition as something Jesus should have foreseen. And yet the mystics of this world, be they Christian, Buddhists or Jews, are all agreed once they are on the same plane. I am convinced there is but one truth and I agree with George Soros that none of us possesses that truth.

But I am speaking here as an artist when I say that intuition is also at play here. My intuition tells me we have lived in Europe for many centuries. We have a very high opinion of ourselves, we have been and have become very proud. We see ourselves as embodying the only true values. This, I believe, is a very dangerous standpoint. What we must learn again is how to be modest and to view the human being from a cosmic perspective as a small particle of dust, as a small entity in the cosmos. Then we will discover that modesty is the first item we must learn to accept. For me, an "open society" is one which recognises that no one possesses the sole truth, which does not mean that this sole truth does not exist. I believe this truth does exist but without our having access to it.

I remember when Chile was ruled by a dictatorship and I was doing a film in Berlin with Chilean refugees. I became really frightened when they told me that torture was neither good or bad. When it is perpetrated by Pinochet, it is reactionary torture, but when we come to power we will torture them and that will be progressive torture and therefore something completely different. I believe torture is always evil, universally evil and that one item in any catalogue of global ethics must be: "Do not torture your neighbour, even if you are in a position to do so." When we recognise this, we can perhaps also accept that future generations will inherit many material things other generations have created.

And yet each individual, each and every person must absorb culture for her or himself. After all, we are all born barbarians and must assimilate our own culture in the course of our lives. We can create global solidarity only if we recognise that people are different yet also the same. Too many people live on our planet; our means of communication are very highly developed. About ten years ago travelling in Africa, I sat in a plane and noticed that white passengers sat in one cabin and black passengers in another. I asked the stewardess why this was so; was it that the computer had divided people in that way? No, no, that is our policy. We are not racists but we know that our comrades like to sit together.

Our world is too small. We can not afford the luxury of sitting only with people who are just like us. We have to strive to reach a level of human consciousness at which we understand that the principle values, if firmly anchored, are also universal values.

This essay is based on a statement made by Kryzstof Zanussi at a public podium discussion on 13 June 1999 in the Vienna Volkstheater on the topic of "Global Ethics – Illusion or Reality?".

Globalisation Requires Cultural Dialogue

Monika Kalista

As we enter the 21st century, all countries will face new challenges with regard to their foreign cultural policy. A globalised world requires above all a greater willingness than ever before to engage in dialogue. This is true for states, regions, groups and individuals.

Aware of this, I believe the purpose of foreign cultural relations today is to promote cultural dialogue. In our day and age, cultures can no longer be misunderstood as belonging to monolithic blocs pitted against each other. This way of thinking would inevitably lead to a "clash of civilisations" of the kind Samuel Huntington described so pessimistically several years ago.

Austrian Foreign Minister Wolfgang Schüssel elaborated on this subject as follows: "Art and culture have the difficult task of always being ahead of their times. Austrian foreign cultural policy must be especially attuned to this aspect as we stand at the threshold of the new millennium. What the times call for is not a cautious reconstruction of international trends but the courage to think beyond current international possibilities. We must adopt this intellectual attitude to complete the great European project of peace that was the goal and the prime motivation for the founding fathers of the European Community."

Building on this fundamental idea, we must devise concepts of modern foreign cultural policy based on the idea of dialogue. Following are several concrete examples showing how this is happening in practice:

The Austrian Foreign Ministry has been staging Christian-Islamic dialogue conferences in Vienna since 1993. Their aim has been to promote greater understanding between the different religions by emphasising common ground and analysing differences in an objective and non-emotional way. The relationships the monotheistic religions have among themselves were discussed in detail at other conference events (e.g. "Europe of Religions"). In the future, we intend to further develop and expand this series of conferences for promoting a dialogue among the religions.

During the Austrian EU Presidency, we were instrumental in supporting the international presentation of the large exhibition project "Islamic Cultural Routes in the Mediterranean." This presentation took place in October 1998 in the Mediterranean Museum in Stockholm, the designated European Cultural Capital that year. The project, developed by the Austrian non-governmental organisation "Museum without Borders" in collaboration with the European Commission and several states of the EUROMED Partnership, takes what I feel is a very interesting approach. Its objective is to present the art of the Mediterranean in a vivid way and thus promote tolerance towards different religions by fostering greater understanding among them.

In September 1998, the Austrian Foreign Ministry joined with the Vienna Eastern and South-eastern European Institute to stage an international conference on the topic of "Multiculturalism and Multi-ethnicity in Central, Eastern and South-eastern Europe." The result of this meeting, the so-called "Vienna Declaration", stresses the significance of those factors in the European enlargement debate that go beyond purely economical key performance figures. The role of culture, religion, language, the media, society and politics is examined and described in precise terms. A follow-up conference on "Multiculturalism" was staged just nine months later in May 1999 at Austria Center Vienna. This event brought together non-governmental organisations from many different parts of the world, with delegates in attendance from Africa, Asia, Australia, and Western and Eastern Europe. The results of this meeting, which focused on civil society, were published in the autumn of 1999.

In August 1999 the Federal Ministry of Foreign Affairs staged a large international symposium in conjunction with the Salzburg Festival. The focal topic of the event was the future of European thought in a globalised world. It was discussed by prominent figures such as the philosopher and mayor of Venice Massimo Cacciari, Peter Sloterdijk, Salzburg Festival Director Gerard Mortier, the Finnish Minister of Culture Suvi Linden as chairwoman of the EU Council of Cultural Ministers, and World Bank Vice President Ismail Serageldin. On the occasion of the Austrian chairmanship of the Organisation for Security and Co-operation in Europe (OSCE), a pilot project entitled "Academy of Good Neighbours" will seek to explore, teach about and discuss the factors individuals and entire peoples require to live together in harmony. In the first phase, academic institutions from Vienna, Graz, Munich, Bratislava, Budapest, Bucharest and Cracow will develop this idea which will later be further expanded to include other partners. Cross-border youth projects will round out the above activities. All of them can be reduced to a single common denominator:

At the dawn of this new millennium, cultural policy must be understood more than ever before as a policy of peace. This is why Austrian foreign cultural policy considers culture and education to be such significant factors, also in the reconstruction now underway in the territory of the former Yugoslavia. The efforts to rebuild roads, bridges, railways and buildings must be accompanied by a cultural, intellectual and thus also moral reconstruction of this important region in Europe. A leading Austrian intellectual and artist once said: "Culture could well become a religion in the 21st century." I do not know if things will go that far, but I am absolutely certain of one thing: The role of art and culture in achieving an open global society characterised by mutual understanding and tolerance is presumably greater today than it has been at any other time in the history of mankind. This thought is a major motivation for us and an important impetus for the diverse activities being undertaken as part of the current Austrian foreign cultural policy.

Building an open global society will take more than a day, more than several years even. However, concerted foreign cultural policy actions by several states, which consistently promote this idea of dialogue, would certainly be important paving stones on the road to this goal. Austria will be a reliable partner in the process.

Vienna Conclusions on Globality and Global Ethics

Compilation by the Conference Drafting Committee
June 12, 1999

At the invitation of the Austrian Federal Ministry for Foreign Affairs (State Secretary for Foreign Affairs Benita Ferrero-Waldner) and with the co-operation of the Department of Canadian Heritage (Secretary of State for Multiculturalism and Status of Women Hedy Fry), intellectuals from a variety of backgrounds met in Vienna on June 11 and 12, 1999. UNESCO was represented by the Director of the Philosophy Department, Yersu Kim and the Director of the Department for Cultural Pluralism, Katérina Stenou. The European Union was represented by the Director of the European Monitoring Centre on Racism and Xenophobia, Beate Winkler. The objective was to share ideas, hopes and concerns related to the development of a global ethic to guide policy makers in meeting the challenges and opportunities which are a result of the globalisation of our societies and economies.

Participants agreed that the notion of a global ethic remains to be defined, but that it must be treated as a permanently dynamic concept; as a work-in-progress.

In recognition of the limited international nature of the participation in the Conference, one of the prime conclusions was that the dialogue around a Global Ethic must be broadened and deepened, it must be "globalised" and democratised to reflect the diversity of the international community. There were many expressions of disappointment over the lack of progress at implementing existing international and national commitments to accommodate plurality in democratic processes and institutions. Participants also agreed with the claim that in many ways the emerging dialogue is in itself an indispensable part of the process. Even in the absence of a more precise definition, participants were reminded by their host, the Austrian State Secretary for Foreign Affairs, that they were dealing with a subject of no less importance than how we choose to live together.

The Conference agenda focused on three inter-related aspects of globality:
- Global Ethics and International Dialogue
- Global Ethics and International Media Society
- Global Ethics and Cultural Pluralism

Recommendations

A principle theme which emerged was the need to build an improved and enduring linkage between intentions and actions. There is a need for implementing those elements of a global ethic which are explicit or implicit in existing international agreements and commitments. The notion of Global Responsibility was employed to characterise the ethic which would ensure the sustainability of the natural and human environment. In the context of moving from passive to active, amongst the recommendations which were proposed were:

1. Intensify the human rights dialogue within and amongst members of the public, governments, civil society, religions, and the business community

2. Strengthening compliance with human rights commitments, with particular attention to sheltering the weak and vulnerable in our societies

3. Strengthen international labour standards and labour law to improve the protection of workers from exploitation

4. Strengthen the cross-cultural capacities of international dispute mechanisms and institutions

5. Take measures to enhance journalistic ethics and the capacity to reinforce public awareness and acceptance of human rights, global ethics and cultural pluralism (e.g. a self-regulating international arrangement within the journalism community, and loosening of employer constraints on media professionals)

6. The apparent uncontrollability of the Internet and its limited access by disadvantaged groups was viewed as a characteristic of globalisation which must be addressed so as not to neutralise its potential for building cross-cultural respect and trust

7. The development of innovative measures to avoid abuse of the Internet and to better exploit its potential for democracy and pluralism was viewed as a priority

8. Create an improved environment for sustaining pluralism of opinion and perspectives in national and international media (e.g. constraints on concentration of ownership and supports for small market media)

9. National and international policies must be conceived and implemented recognising that cultural plurality is a permanent and positive characteristic of globalised society, to be nurtured and built upon

10. Vulnerable peoples and endangered languages and cultures will require a variety of sheltering and nourishing techniques in order to ensure their sustainability

11. Education for pluralism and human rights is a precondition for establishing a global ethic. Maintaining the capacity of the world languages and cultures to utilise the new technologies and to communicate the arguments for pluralism must be a prime objective of contemporary education.

Authors

Ernst-Peter Brezovszky
Born in Innsbruck in 1961
Minister at the Austrian Federal Ministry of Foreign Affairs, Vienna; since autumn 1999, Austrian consul general in Cracow

Rudolf Burger, professor
Born in Vienna in 1938
Chairman of the Department of Philosophy, Rector of the School of Applied Arts, Vienna

Benita Ferrero – Waldner
Born in Salzburg in 1948
State Secretary at the Austrian Federal Ministry of Foreign Affairs, Vienna

Hedy Fry
Secretary of State for Multiculturalism and the Status of Women at the Ministry for Canadian Heritage, Ottawa

Sakej Youngblood Henderson, professor
Research Director of the Native Law Centre (diplomatic training center for indigenous legal experts and research institute for legal systems) at the University of Saskatchewan

Monika Kalista
Born in Salzburg in 1948
Director Gerneral for Cultural Affairs in the Austrian Federal Ministry of Foreign Affairs, Vienna

Hanspeter Neuhold, professor
Born in Budapest in 1942
Chairman of the Institute for International Law, University of Vienna

Ebenezer Njoh-Mouelle, professor
Born in Yaoundé
Professor of Philosophy, University of Yaoundé, Cameroon
Several years as presidential advisor, Member of the Executive Board of UNESCO

Peter Pelinka
Born in Vienna in 1951
Editor-in-chief of the Austrian news magazine *News*
Host of the weekly ORF political panel discussion *Zur Sache*
Teaching position in journalism at the University of Vienna

George Soros
Born in Budapest in 1930
Finance expert and philanthropist, New York

Arnold Suppan, professor
Born in St. Veit in 1945
President of the Austrian Institute of Eastern and Southeastern European Studies
Professor at the Institute for East European History, University of Vienna

Andreas Unterberger
Born in Vienna in 1949
Editor-in-chief of the Austrian daily newspaper *Die Presse*, Vienna

Beate Winkler
Born in Dresden in 1949
Director of the European Monitoring Centre on Racism and Xenophobia, Vienna

Alexander Wrabetz
Born in Vienna in 1960
Business Director of the ORF (Austrian Broadcasting Company), Vienna

Krzysztof Zanussi
Born in Warsaw
Film director and script writer
Director of TOR State Film Studios, Warsaw